はじめに

住宅、公共建築、商業施設などを幅広く手がけ、世界も注目する気鋭の建築家・平田晃久(1971-)の展覧会を開催します。1985年の開館以来、日本の近・現代美術を主な対象領域としてきた練馬区立美術館では、初の建築展です。この後、当館はコレクション展の開催を経て改築工事の準備に入るため、本展は既存の建物全館を使って実施する最後の企画展でもあります。新館の建築設計を担っている平田さんの建築展をもって、新旧の美術館をつなぐ架け橋とすることができればと願っています。

有機的なフォルムを特徴とする平田さんの建築は、「からまりしろ」という自らが作った造語によって、その論理性や合理性をうかがい知ることができます。「からまる」と「しろ(余白)」を組み合わせることにより、かちっと囲い取られた四角い空間ではなく、もっとあいまいで複雑なすきまやひだをもった場所を作る。平田さんは、そこに建築の新しい理想を見出そうとしているようです。一本の樹の上に、数百の種類の生き物が共存し、生態系を形づくっているように、自然環境のような建築を作ることはできないかという平田建築の挑戦は続きます。

平田さんは、伊東豊雄建築設計事務所を経て2005年に独立。2008年の住宅「イエノイエ」が実際に建った最初の住宅建築となりました。住宅の1/1模型ともいえるこの建物は、特異な形状の屋根が印象的で、山脈の尾根と谷という自然の形態になぞらえた屋根の造りとなっています。「住宅を、複数の独立した個人がスペースを共有する建物ととらえると、一人になれる場所も欲しい。ヒダ状に展開する空間ならば、オープンな場所とクローズドな場所を滑らかに展開させることができる」(註)と平田さんは設計の狙いを明らかにしています。

その後、平田さんは「ヴェネチア・ビエンナーレ国際建築展2012」に参加、伊東豊雄日本館コミッショナーのもとで、建築家の乾久美子と藤本壮介、写真家の畠山直哉の各氏とともに、陸前高田市に「みんなの家」を建てる過程を展覧会として視覚化しました。「みんなの家」は、仮設住宅での生活を余儀なくされた東日本大震災の被災者の方々が自由に集まり、語らうことができるささやかな憩いの場を作ろうと伊東さんが始めたプロジェクトです。建築作品でもアートでもない、プリミティブな公共建築を作るという伊東コミッショナーの意に賛同し、平田さんはコミュニティ再生へ

の想いから2人の建築家と協働、陸前高田に「みんなの家」を完成させました。竣工に先立ち開幕したヴェネチア・ビエンナーレ日本館の展示は、建築とは何かという根源的な意味を問い直すことの勇気と重要さが評価され、最高賞である金獅子賞を受賞しています。

「みんなの家」で示された、コミュニティの中へと深く入っていき、住民の方々の声に耳を傾ける姿勢は、平田さんの代表的建築のひとつとなった太田市美術館・図書館におけるワークショップの手法へとつながり、深化を遂げたのではないかと推察しています。同館の設計においては、ワークショップは単なる意見を聞く場ではなく、基本設計を具体化していく議論の場として活用され、のべ7回のワークショップと300の模型制作を経て、みんなで作った美術館・図書館が2017年に誕生しました。同館は、美術館と図書館がからまり、街や緑ともからまっており、まるで街のなかを回遊するかのように内部を楽しく歩き回れる空間となっています。オープンな場所とクローズドな場所をからませた「イエノイエ」と同様、この公共施設においても、利用者はそれぞれ自分の場を見つけて、自分の時間を過ごすことができるような工夫が施されており、利用者に心地よさを提供しているように思われます。

新しい美術館像を提示した太田における試みは、ここ練馬区立美術館・貫井図書館の新館設計においても、より大きなスケールのもとで、発展的に生かされていくものと期待は高まるばかりです。美術館と図書館による単なる空間の共有・共存にとどまらず、新施設は多様な活動を通した有機的な連携を模索しています。美術館に求められる役割や機能は時代とともに多様化しており、まちづくりや国際交流、観光・産業のほか、社会的・地域的課題と向き合う役割も期待されるほどに拡張へ向かっています。とはいえ、調査研究、資料の収集・保存、展示・教育普及という美術館の基本的使命は揺らぐことはありません。新しく拡張していく機能と、美術館の基盤となる部分、この両者をデザインと運用の両面でどのようにからめて、21世紀的な美術館の実現をはかるのか、多数の方々を巻き込みながら、計画は進行中です。

本展は、平田さんの20年にわたる建築活動の節目となった上述の4つのプロジェクトをはじめ、これまでの建築作品の数々と、様々な事情により実現しなかった建物、現在進行中のプロジェクトなどを取り上げ、建築模型、図面、ドローイング、写真、関連資料等を

3つのテーマに散りばめて展示いたします。また各展示室をつなぐ
ロビーを中心に、半透明な布によるインスタレーションも計画され
ており、ニュートラルな美術館の空間に楔を打ち込むものとなるで
しょう。展覧会のタイトル「人間の波打ちぎわ」は、平田さん自身
の命名によるもので、自然や環境との結節点にある建築と、そこを
ベースに暮らし活動する人間との関係性を示唆しているのではな
いかと私は思います。すべてが自然に通じていることを裏書きする
ような平田建築の世界を観客の皆さんにご体感いただき、本展が
未来へ向けた建築のあり方について改めて考える機会となれば幸
いです。

本展の開催にあたりましては、平田晃久氏、並びに同建築設計事
務所のスタッフの方々から多大なご協力をいただきました。この
場を借りて心より御礼申し上げます。また貴重な作品をご出品くだ
さった所蔵者の皆様、ご後援、ご助成、ご協賛賜りました関係各
位、そして本展の実現に向けてご尽力くださった多数の関係者に
深く感謝の意を表します。

伊東正伸（練馬区立美術館　館長）

註：
『日経アーキテクチュア』2008年10月27日号、54頁

Foreword

It is with great pleasure that we present an exhibition showcasing the highly innovative and internationally recognized architect Akihisa Hirata (b. 1971), known for an extensive portfolio including residential, public, and commercial projects. This is the first architecture exhibition at the Nerima Art Museum, which opened in 1985 and has primarily focused on Japanese modern and contemporary art. The exhibition is also a turning point for the museum as its last special exhibition utilizing the entire building (to be followed by a show of works from the permanent collection) before closing for demolition and construction of a new building. This exhibition of Hirata's work is particularly significant in that he is the designer of the museum's new building, and it is envisioned as a bridge symbolically linking the museum's old and new structures.

Hirata's architecture, distinguished by its organic forms, can be interpreted through the neologism *karamishiro* (lit. "tangling base"), which he coined to describe his design ethos. The combination of "tangling" and "base" describes how Hirata strives to create not rigidly defined rectilinear spaces but more ambiguous and complex ones, replete with gaps and folds. This approach embodies his aspirations toward a new architectural ideal. His vision evokes the coexistence of hundreds of species within a single tree's ecosystem, and he continually challenges himself to design structures that echo the intricacies of natural environments.

After his tenure at Toyo Ito & Associates, Architects, Hirata established his own practice in 2005. His 2008 project Ie no Ie (House of Houses) marked his first foray into residential architecture. The building could be said to resemble a 1:1 model of a house, with a distinctive roof that mimics the natural contours of mountain ridges and valleys. Hirata has articulated his design intentions as follows: "If you view a dwelling as a structure in which multiple independent individuals share space, there should be places for solitude. Spaces that incorporate folds facilitate smooth transitions between open and closed areas."*

Hirata subsequently participated in the 2012 Venice Biennale of Architecture, where Toyo Ito served as commissioner of the Japan Pavilion. He joined architects Kumiko Inui and Sou Fujimoto and photographer Naoya Hatakeyama in realizing an exhibit that conveyed the construction of Home-for-All in Rikuzentakata City. Initiated by Ito, Home-for-All was a project that aimed to provide a modest gathering space for those displaced into temporary housing by the Great East Japan Earthquake, a place where survivors could freely assemble, relax, and communicate. Empathizing with Commissioner Ito's vision for a primitive form of public architecture that transcends both merely functional and purely aesthetic architecture or art, Hirata collaborated with the other architects and the local community to bring Home-for-All to fruition in Rikuzentakata. This endeavor, unveiled at the Venice Biennale of Architecture's Japan Pavilion before the project was completed, fundamentally rethought the essence of architecture and received the Golden Lion Award, the Biennale's highest honor, for its daring and significance.

The approach demonstrated in Home-for-All, entailing deep engagement with the community and attentive listening to residents' needs, has evidently evolved and deepened, including through Hirata's subsequent workshops relating to the Art Museum & Library, Ota, one of the architect's representative works. These workshops transcended mere sessions for exchanges of opinion, becoming platforms for discussion that shaped the basic design of the facility. After seven workshops and the fabrication of 300 models, a collaboratively designed museum and library came to fruition in 2017. The art museum and library "tangle" with each other, and with the city and the natural environment, resulting in a space that encourages exploration and enjoyment, reminiscent of wandering through a city. Echoing Ie no Ie, which mingled open and closed areas, this public facility allows users to find their own personal spaces, enhancing their comfort and well-being.

Anticipation is rising for the larger-scale, more

advanced application of this innovative approach, piloted in Ota, to the design of the new building here at the Nerima Art Museum and Nukui Library. The goal for this facility is not only to have the museum and library to coexist and share space, but also to foster organic synergies through various activities. The roles and functions expected of museums are expanding and evolving to encompass urban development, international exchange, tourism, industry, and addressing social and regional challenges. At the same time, the core missions of museums – to conduct research, acquire and preserve artworks and materials, and offer exhibitions and educational outreach – remain unchanged. The ongoing challenge lies in integrating these expanding roles with the fundamental aspects of museums through both design and operation, striving to create a 21st-century museum that involves numerous stakeholders in its ongoing development.

This exhibition marks a significant milestone in Hirata's 20-year architectural career. It features not only the four aforementioned major projects but also a broad array of other architectural works, projects that went unrealized due to various circumstances, and current initiatives in progress. The exhibits include architectural models, drawings, sketches, photographs, and related materials, organized into three thematic sections. In addition, a striking installation consisting of translucent fabric is planned for the lobby that connects the galleries, enlivening the museum's neutral space. The exhibition, titled *Architecture Arises at the Water's Edge for Humans* by Hirata himself, explores the relationship between architecture, which intersects with nature and the environment, and people who build their lives and activities around architectural spaces. It is our hope that this exhibition provides visitors with profound insights into Hirata's architectural vision, underscoring his emphasis on universal connections with nature and prompting reconsideration of the future possibilities of architecture.

We are immensely grateful to Akihisa Hirata and the staff of his architectural practice for their extensive cooperation in organizing this exhibition. We also extend our deepest gratitude to the collectors who have lent their valuable works for display, as well as to all of those whose sponsorship, support, cooperation, and tireless efforts have made this exhibition a reality.

Masanobu Ito
Director, Nerima Art Museum

Note:
*Quote reprinted from *Nikkei Architecture*, October 27, 2008, p. 54

凡例

・本書は「平田晃久―人間の波打ちぎわ」展の図録兼書籍として制作された。

・展覧会は、「第1章 からましろ―身体の波打ちぎわ」、「第2章 響き―意識の波打ちぎわ」、「第3章 響きの響き―時空の波打ちぎわ」で
　構成されるが、本書はそれに準じたものではない。

・展覧会には、50件のプロジェクトが紹介されているが、本書ではその内の21件を掲載している。

・pp. 16-131のテキストは、平田晃久が執筆した。

・美術館での展覧会風景写真を掲載している（pp. 137-145）。

・展覧会の出品物については、巻末に出品リストを掲載している。

・作品解説は、平田晃久建築設計事務所が執筆した。

・翻訳は、川上純子（pp. 8-131）、クリストファー・スティヴンズ（pp. 2-5、pp. 134-136、pp. 149-161）による。

Notes

· This book serves as a catalogue for the exhibition "AKIHISA HIRATA: Architecture Arises at the Water's Edge for Humans".

· This exhibition is divided into three chapters: 1. Karamarishiro: The Water's Edge for Human / 2. Reverberations: The Water's
　Edges for the Consciousness / 3. Reverberations of Reverberations: The Water's Edge of Space-Time, however it doesn't
　necessarily appear in the order of display at the exhibition in this book.

· This exhibition presents 50 projects, but this book appears 21 projects.

· Texts for project page were written by Akihisa Hirata.

· This book appears installation views at the Nerima Art Museum (pp. 137-145).

· The list of works is included at the end of the catalogue.

· The explanation of the works were written by akihisa hirata architecture office.

· Texts were translated into English by Junko Kawakami (pp. 8-131), and Christopher Stephens (pp. 2-5, pp. 134-136, pp. 149-161).

Contents

2	はじめに 伊東正伸		4	Foreword Masanobu Ito
8	平田晃久の建築 西沢立衛		10	Architecture of Akihisa Hirata Ryue Nishizawa
12	人間の波打ちぎわ 平田晃久		14	Architecture Arises at the Water's Edge for Humans Akihisa Hirata

16 **21 Projects at the Water's Edge**

桝屋本店
Architecture Farm
Bloomberg Pavillion
Global Bowl
富富話合
Tree-ness House
Taipei Complex
新竹市中央図書館
Sendai Tree
太田市美術館・図書館
Overlap House
まえばしガレリア
HARAKADO
八代市民俗伝統芸能伝承館
ホントカ。小千谷市ひと・まち・文化共創拠点
シャイニング・クラウズ
BIG-TREE
Cloud and Field
EXPO ナショナルデーホール「レイガーデン」
臺灣大學 藝文大樓
練馬区立美術館・貫井図書館

16 **21 Projects at the Water's Edge**

Masuya
Architecture Farm
Bloomberg Pavillion
Global Bowl
Taipei Roofs
Tree-ness House
Taipei Complex
Knowledge Canyon
Sendai Tree
Art Museum & Library, Ota
Overlap House
Maebashi Galleria
HARAKADO
Center of Yatsushiro Folk Performing Arts
HONTOKA。Ojiya City People, Town, Cultural Co-creation Base
Shining Clouds
BIG-TREE
Cloud and Field
EXPO National Day Hall "Ray Garden"
Theater, Art Gallery and Museum of Taiwan university
Nerima Art Museum and Nukui Library

132	平面図		132	Plan
134	解説・概要データ		134	Explanation and Data
137	展覧会風景		137	Installation Views at the Nerima Art Museum
146	展覧会出品リスト		146	List of Works
149	100年後の美術館を想像して 小野寛子		153	Envisioning the Museum a Century from Now Hiroko Ono
157	練馬の富士塚をめぐる 根岸博之		159	The Fujizuka of Nerima Hiroyuki Negishi
162	平田晃久プロジェクトデータ		162	Data on Works since 2003
165	プロフィール、スタッフリスト		165	Profile, Staff of akihisa hirata architecture office

平田晃久の建築

平田さんは今の日本の建築界を代表する建築家の一人であり、きわめて先鋭的かつ創造的な仕事をしている建築家として、国内外で広く知られている。平田さんが独立して間もない頃に台湾で手がけた住宅＊が登場した時のことは、今もよく覚えている。私はそれを一目で好きになった。理由はいくつもあるが、まず第一に、それは現実の空間でありかつ理念的な空間でもあることだった。そこには、現実と理念が一体化したかというような驚きがあった。その理念、違う言い方をすれば理念空間モデルと言ってもいいかもしれないが、どういう空間モデルかというと、一言で言えば「生成」と呼びたくなるものだ。なにかひとつの出来事なり事故なりが最初にあって、そこから瞬く間に形が生まれ育ってゆく。生成の概念が建築の形ひとつで説明されている。生成概念の建築化ということだ。それが、私がこの建築を好きな第二の理由だ。この生成は偶然的でもあるし必然的でもあるし、関数的なものでもあるかもしれない。自動的と言うとさすがに語弊があるかもしれないが、その生成運動は作家がデザインした通りに動く運動ではなくて、作家の意図を超えようとする運動だ。ここに私が好きな第三点目がある。つまりこの建築には美学的な部分がない、という点だ。ないというか、もちろんないことはないが、美しいかどうかの価値基準が動力源になっていない。それは美しさを目指していない運動で、違う言い方をすれば、なにかまるでゴールがないかのようだ。何に向かって育っていくか誰もわからないという開放性と暴力性がある。ここで私がこの建築に注目する第四点は、それは理念空間モデルというきわめて抽象的な存在でありながら、なにか言いようもない過剰さがあるという点だ。その過剰さがなんなのかよくわからないが、わかりやすい比喩でいえば、それは平田さんご本人にお会いしたときに、ご本人のオーラから感じるものにかなり近いそれだ。きわめて理念的で抽象化された建築であるにも関わらず、省略できない過剰さが、建築にまとわりついている。きわめて鋭利で形而上学的な知性を持ちながら華麗なファッションをまとって笑いをとる平田さんの人格と肉体が、そのまま建築に転化しているように感じてしまう。平田さんご本人を見るたびに、この建築の過剰さは飾りではなくて、必須のものなのだと私は感じている。

　私は「太田市美術館・図書館」も好きだ。私はこの建築を、平田さんが台湾で試みたことの展開の一つと見ている。それは、取り付く島もないような真っ平で広大な関東平野の只中で、うわっと渦巻き状に出来事が立体化していくといったような感じの建築である。世の中にはいろいろな建築があるが、中にはたまに、外観だけを見て、その中に入る必要がない建築というものがある。入らなくてもその創造性がわかってしまう建築があって、「太田市美術館・図書館」はそれだった。関係性がそのまま形になっている。中も外もないというか、中がそのまま外になったと言ってもいいかもしれない。また、それとまったく矛盾することを言ってしまうが、過剰な外観がある。いくら理念的モデルと言われても、理念の一語にはおさまりようのない過剰性がまとわりついており、それを見ていると、理念的なものがそのまま社会的なものでもあるという、抽象化されたものがそのまま人間でもあるというような発想が、そこにある

気がしてくる。平田さんの建築はいつも、先ほど私が空間モデルと呼んだ、きわめて抽象的で観念的なものと、きわめて表現的で世俗的なものが一体化したというような建築だ。それは前述の二プロジェクトに限ったことではなくて、その二つはたまたまの事例であって、平田さんの作品ほぼすべてに言えることではないかと私は感じている。平田さんは建築設計の場で、理念的な空間モデルを構想する。しかしそれがどれだけ抽象的なものであったとしても、なお平田さんの人格が現れる。どれだけ抽象化してもなお残る人間の姿、という言い方もできるし、または逆に、抽象化を目指すからこそ、そこに人間が現れるのかもしれない。

　しかしそういえば私は、平田さんが伊東豊雄さんの事務所に勤務していた頃から、それに近いようなことを平田さんに感じていたかもしれない。当時平田さんが担当していたプロジェクトを見て、私はそこに平田さんの世界があると感じていたかもしれない。あの頃すでに、平田さんの現在の仕事につながるような、現実の建築でありながら理念モデルでもあるというような、かつ、抽象的なものと過剰なものが一体であるというような、抽象性と具体性の一体感があった。そこはまた平田さんの、別のすごいところでもあって、平田さんが修行時代に一担当スタッフとしてやってきたことと、今自分の名前でもってやっている仕事とが、ほとんどそのまま連続している。修行中であるとか一人でやるとか、そういう自分の立場が何かに関わらず、平田さんの創造性というものはもうそこに確固としてあるのだ。そういう建築家は、私の周りには平田さん以外にいない。

西沢立衛

* 「Architecture Farm」

Architecture of Akihisa Hirata

One of Japan's leading architects today, Mr. Hirata is widely known both in Japan and overseas as an architect whose designs are extremely radical and creative. I still remember when the house in Taiwan* he designed soon after he had become independent was published. I instantly fell for it. There are many reasons why, but the first is that it was actual space as well as conceptual space. To my surprise, the actual and the conceptual were integrated. In a nutshell, the concept—it would be safe to say it is a conceptual spatial model—is something that could be called a spatial model of "becoming." In the model, there is an event or an accident at the beginning, which instantly evokes and develops a form. The concept of becoming is represented by that architectural form alone. In other words, it represents the architecturalization of the concept of becoming. This is the second reason why I like this building. This becoming is accidental as well as inevitable, and it may also be parametric. While it may not be proper to say that it is automatic, the action of becoming is not an action in accordance with the author's design but an action that goes beyond the author's intention. This is the third reason why I like this house. That is, this architectural work has no component intended for aesthetic beauty. Well, no, one may find a few parts that are beautiful, but the design is not driven by aesthetic value. The house embodies an action that does not aim for beauty, and in other words, as if it were an end-less action. It has openness and violence in the sense that nobody knows in which direction it will develop. Here, the fourth reason why I am focusing on this architecture, is that despite being a conceptual spatial model that is a highly abstract existence, the house somehow has indescribable excess. I do not really know what that excessiveness is, but if I put it in a simple analogy, it is something very similar to what I feel in the aura Mr. Hirata emanates when I see him in person. Though the house is a project that is highly conceptual and abstract, a kind of excess that cannot be reduced clings to it. I feel that the personality and physical existence of Mr. Hirata, who is always dressed in gorgeous outfits, has an extremely keen and metaphysical mind and loves to get a laugh from others, are simply transformed into this architecture. Whenever I see him in person, I feel that the excessiveness of this architecture is not something ornamental but essential.

I also like the Art Museum & Library, Ota. In my opinion, this building is a development of what he tried to do in the house in Taiwan. Right in the middle of nowhere, on the vast Kanto Plain, it seems as if events were swept into a dynamic spiral that eventually became a building, a three-dimensional entity. There are various kinds of buildings in this world, and occasionally, it is enough to see them from the outside and you do not need to go inside. There are buildings whose unique creativity can be seen even without entering, and that is the case for the Art Museum & Library, Ota. The form was derived from relationships. There is no distinction between the interior and exterior. It is probably safe to say that the exterior was directly derived from the interior. In direct contradiction with what I have just written, the façade looks excessive. No matter how conceptual the model is, the excess that cannot be confined in the conceptual clings to the building, and when I see it, I get the impression that behind it are the ideas that the conceptual is also the social and that the abstract is the human. In Mr. Hirata's architectural creations, the extremely abstract and conceptual—what I called the spatial model earlier—and the extremely expressive and worldly are integrated. I feel that this is true not only for the two projects I mentioned earlier, examples that were chosen for this article, but for almost every Hirata work. When designing a building, he creates a conceptual spatial model. But however abstract it is, it still represents his personality. It can be said that it is a human quality that remains no matter how abstract his model is. To put it another way, just because he pursues abstraction, a human quality arises.

In retrospect, however, I may have felt something similar to this ever since he was a member of Toyo Ito's studio staff. When I saw the projects he was in charge of, I may have recognized his originality in them. There was already a unity of the abstract and the concrete that would lead to his current projects, in which actual buildings are conceptional models and the abstract and the excessive are integrated. This is another exceptional thing about Mr. Hirata, since most of the work he does today under his own name is developed in direct continuity with the work he did during his apprentice days. Regardless of his status—whether as an apprentice or an independent architect—his creativity was already firmly established. There is no other architect like that around me, except for Mr. Hirata.

Ryue Nishizawa

*Architecture Farm

人間の波打ちぎわ

平田晃久

私たちは「人間」というものが、生命の世界につながり、変容してゆく時代を生きている。建築も変容してゆくだろう。しかし新しい建築は、近代が前提としていた人間像の少し外側ー人間の波打ちぎわーにはみ出そうとするときにのみ、姿を表すのではないか。

これまでのところ、僕はさしあたり3つの「人間の波打ちぎわ」に近づき、そこから新しい建築を見つけようとしてきたように思う。それはこの度の展覧会における、3つの展示室での展示と対応している。

Ⅰ. からまりしろー身体の波打ちぎわ

幼い頃、昆虫少年だった僕は、蝶のような、蟷螂のような、蝉のような眼になって、野山を歩きまわった。建築物のつくり出す人工的な環境と、虫たちのいる自然環境はどうしてこんなに違うのだろうか。

花々のあいだの複雑な隙間を、蝶たちが自由に乗りこなすように、私たちも自由に動き、動物の一種として、豊かな環境の広がりを感じながら生きてゆきたい。

一本の樹の上に、さまざまな生物が絡まり、生態系を形づくっているように、建築も自然環境のような、人々が自由に絡まるものになれるだろうか。〈からまりしろ〉という言葉は、絡まる＋しろ（＝余白）という意味の造語だ。花々の隙間は蝶にとってのからまりしろ、叢は蟷螂や蝗にとっての、樹木は蝉や蜥蜴や栗鼠や鳥や苔にとってのからまりしろである。そしてもし、建築が人々や他の生物たちのからまりしろ、なのだとしたら？

人間も他の動物たちと同じように身体を持ち、環境と絡まり合う存在である。からまりしろの建築は、そんな動物としての身体の波打ちぎわに現れる。そんな自然環境のような場所は、私たちが考えたり行動したりする能力を押し拡げ活性化させるだろう。動物としての私たちの脳は自然環境の中で進化したのだから。

Ⅱ. 響きー意識の波打ちぎわ

ところで、植物たちも知性を持ち、揮発性の物質を介して会話しているそうだ。それぞれ特定のメッセージを帯びた物質が、あたかも特定の色がついた雲や煙のように拡がり、無数の色の雲が重なり合うような世界を、植物たちは生きている。

それは、言葉を介した人間のコミュニケーションとは異なるけれど、もっと古くから生命の世界で交わされてきたものだ。私たちが知っているもので言うと、それは香りとか音の響きの知覚に近いのだろう。こうしたありようを〈響き〉と呼んでみる。

人間活動の集積もまた、〈響き〉を発生させている。たとえば東京の夜景。ひとつひとつの建物は人間的な意図でできているのに、それらが集積し響き合うと、細胞の中を覗き込んだような、うごめく世界が現れる。人間たちの思いが無数に重なり合って、集合的無意識のようなものが形成される時、その響きに耳を傾けながら建築をつくることができるかもしれない。コンピュータは、このような〈響き〉を可視化しはじめている。それはいわば意識の波打ちぎわである。安定した自意識を前提とした近代的作家性が揺らぐところで、集合的無意識の響きと対話しながら、建築を設計すること。

Ⅲ. 響きの響きー時空の波打ちぎわ

しかしそうすると、これからの建築は、意識と無意識の波打ちぎわ、人間の意識にのぼらないものたちの響きの中に、溶けていくだけなのだろうか。

もう一つ、考えていることがある。今を生きる私たちが奏でる〈響き〉がある意味で現世的だとすれば、それとは全く異なる〈響き〉をそこに重ねることだ。今ではないいつか、ここではないどこか、私ではない誰かからやって来る〈響き〉が、現世的な〈響き〉と重なる時、そこには高次の〈響きの響き〉が生まれるだろう。

たとえば、練馬の美術館・図書館の設計において、「富士塚」のことに触れ、富士山を遠く離れたところから見続けてきた人々の意識と、現代の人々の多様な活動を共存させようとしたのも、そんな考えからだ。多層的な響きを持つ建築によって、アートや本の周りに発生する多様な活動と、この街に生きる人々の日常や、長い時間の中で引き継がれてきたものが、さまざまな差異を孕みながら隣接し、共存する。

時空の波打ちぎわからやって来るような〈響き〉。それは歴史というものを思わせるけれど、物語として記され確立されたものというよりは、どこか感覚的で曖昧なものだ。1000年をこえるような時の中で、多様に引き継がれ、変容してきた感受性のようなものを、現代の建築に引き込むこと。

人間を動物的本能を持った存在として見直す、身体の波打ちぎわ。そこでは〈からまりしろ〉という概念が導き手となった。

　人間が個として思考している内容を超えて、それらが集まるときにだけ現れる、意識の波打ちぎわ。私ではない誰か、ここではないどこか、今ではないいつかが流れ込んでくる時空の波打ちぎわ。そこでは、〈響き〉という言葉が示唆を与える。

　からまりと響き。これらは、近代建築を揺るぎないものにしていた人間のありようを揺るがせるべく、僕たちが手に入れた鍵だ。

　僕たちはこれからも、人間の波打ちぎわの向こう側にある、未来の建築の可能性を探し続けるだろう。自然界のコミュニケーションやAIと私たちの知性が絡み合いながら共存する未来を、想像し続けるだろう。

Architecture Arises at the Water's Edge for Humans

Akihisa Hirata

We are living in an age in which human beings are connected once again to other living beings and are being transformed together. Architecture will also be transformed. However, I think a new architecture will take shape when it goes a bit beyond the expectations for human beings as assumed by modernity—this is what I would call the "water's edge" for human beings.*

Until this point, I have tried to find a new architecture by approaching three types of water's edge, and they are shown in the three corresponding galleries of this exhibition.

I. *Karamarishiro*: The Water's Edge for the Body

As a kid who loved insects, I often went into the mountains and fields and observed the world through the eyes of butterflies, mantises and cicadas. I would wonder, and still wonder, why the artificial environment created by buildings was so different from the natural environment where insects live.

It would be great if we, a type of animal ourselves, could move freely and feel the expanse and richness of the environment, just like the butterflies who freely navigate the complex gaps among the flowers.

Many species live in and around a single tree, as if they are entangled with it, creating an ecosystem. In the same way as the natural environment, would it be possible to create a building in and around which people connect and intermingle with each other? To describe this concept, I coined the portmanteau *karamarishiro*, by combining the words *karamaru* (to entangle, intermingle and connect) and *shiro* (a base). Gaps among flowers create an entangling base for butterflies, as does a tuft of grass for mantises and grasshoppers, and a tree for cicadas, lizards, squirrels and moss. What if a building could create an entangling base for both people and other living beings?

Humans, like other animals, have physical bodies, and interact with their environment. A building that creates an entangling base arises at the water's edge of these physical bodies. A built place that has the quality of a natural environment would expand and invigorate our capabilities to think and act. The human brain has evolved as the human animal has interacted with the natural environment.

II. Reverberations: The Water's Edge for the Consciousness

Plants also have consciousness and talk to each other through volatile substances they emit. Plants live in a world where substances that transmit specific messages, spread out as if they were clouds or smoke of specific colors—it is a world where clouds of countless colors overlap.

The way plants communicate with each other is different from human communication using language, but as living beings, they have done this since primeval times. In terms of what we know, it is probably similar to the perception of smells and sounds. I call these invisible ways of communication "reverberations."

The accumulation of human activities also generates reverberations. One example is the nightscape of Tokyo. While each building was constructed according to the intentions of those who created it, when accumulated they resonate with each other and create a world that seems to be moving, as if we are looking inside a cell. When the myriad overlapping thoughts of human beings form something like a collective unconscious, we may be able to create architecture while listening to its reverberations. Computers have already been visualizing these reverberations, which is the water's edge for our consciousness. I design buildings by communicating with reverberations of collective consciousness. Modern authorship, which assumes a stable sense of self as an individual creator, has already become shaky.

III. Reverberations of Reverberations: The Water's Edge of Space-Time

If that is true, will the architecture of the future dissolve into the water's edge between the unconscious and the conscious, that is, into reverberations of what never surfaces to the conscious mind?

I have another thought. If the reverberations we generate at the moment are something worldly, we may be able to add completely different, otherworldly reverberations. When reverberations from a time that is not the present, from somewhere other than here and from someone else are added to reverberations of this world, higher-order reverberations—that is, reverberations of reverberations—will be generated.

That is why, when designing the museum and library in Nerima, I incorporated the concept of *Fujizuka*, a manmade mound from which to enjoy the view of Mt. Fuji from a distance, many of which were built in the Edo period (1603-1867) to resemble Mt. Fuji. I wanted to create a coexistence between the collective consciousness of local people from the past, who observed and appreciated Mr. Fuji from afar for generations, and the diverse activities of the locals of today. In this polyphonic architecture, a variety of activities that occur around art pieces and books, the everyday life of people and what has been passed down to them for ages coexist, even though they are different in many ways.

Here, the reverberations sound as if they're coming from the water's edge of space-time. Some may think that it is history, but as I see it, it is somewhat sensuous and ambiguous, rather than history as a story that has been written and established. My ambition is to bring into contemporary architecture a sensibility that has been passed down and transformed for more than a thousand years.

At the water's edge for the body, human beings are rediscovered as having animal instincts. The concept of *karamarishiro* (entangling base) is essential to thinking about architecture in this regard.

The water's edge of the consciousness arises only when the collective consciousness goes beyond individual thinking. Someone else, who is not me, somewhere other than here, at a time that is not present drifts to the water's edge of time-space. Here, reverberations become the source of inspiration for architecture.

Entangling and resonating—they are the two keys we obtained to shake up the human condition that has made modern architecture unshakable.

We will continue searching for possibilities for future architecture beyond the water's edge for human beings. We will be imagining a future in which communications in the natural environment, AI and the human intellect coexist.

*My concept of "the water's edge" was inspired by the following two sentences I like:

"Man would be erased, like a face drawn in the sand at the edge of the sea." —Michel Foucault, *The Order of Things*.

"I do not know what I may appear to the world, but to myself I seem to have been only like a boy playing on the seashore, and diverting myself in now and then finding a smoother pebble or a prettier shell than ordinary, whilst the great ocean of truth lay all undiscovered before me." —Isaac Newton, as cited in David Brewster, *Memoirs of the Life, Writings and Discoveries of Sir Isaac Newton*.

人間を動物的本能を持った動く存在として捉えると、どんな建築が生まれるだろうか。
グリッドの壁が斜めにカットされたこの建築は、歩く度に刻一刻と見えるものが変化する森の中の
ような空間を持つ。

斜めラインは直線的だが、それをガイドに立体的な空間のひだが生まれ、経験としては曲線的になる。
多声的な音楽のように、あらゆる方向に身体をとり巻く場所たちが動きの中で現れ、移り変わってゆく。

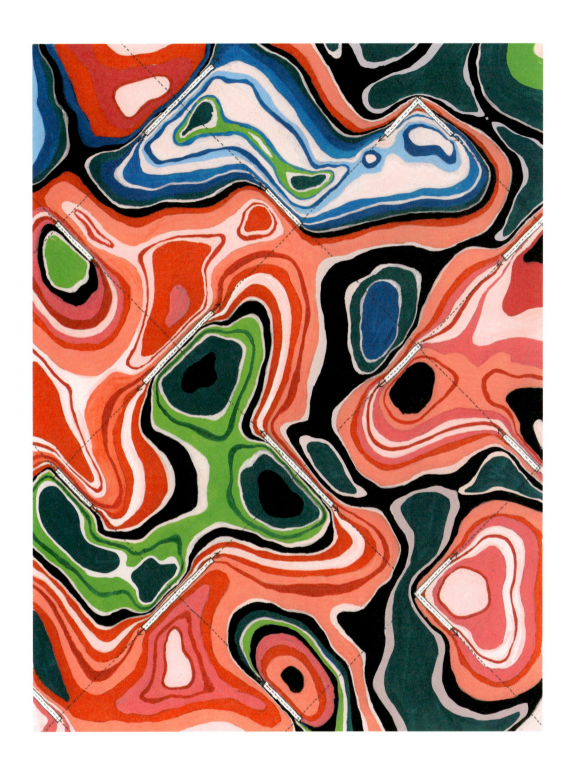

With a view to creating architectural space for humans as beings with animal instincts and mobility, what would be possible? In and around this building, with walls that are diagonally cut, one experiences space like a forest that offers something different each moment as you walk. The diagonals are linear, but crafted in three-dimensional pleats that create the experience of a curvilinear space. Like a piece of polyphonic music, phenomenological places arise around the body in all directions, and they come and go as you move.

たとえばキャベツの葉と葉のあいだ、線香の煙、海中の珊瑚…。
自然界にはひだが満ちている。独立した頃は暇で、そんな形が生成される
幾何学的原理を何に結びつくともわからないままスタディしていた。

Between the leaves of a head of cabbage, in the trails of incense smoke, or the corals in the sea—pleats are found everywhere in nature. When I set up my own studio, I spent my spare time conducting studies on the geometrical principles that create those forms, without knowing what they would lead to.

In a natural setting, pleats emerge around an entity with a limited volume to maximize its surface area. Would it be possible to apply the same principle to architecture? We create architecture to maximize the surface area of limited sites for the sake of human activities. As a result, this building that includes a variety of relationships and catalysts was created. This idea led me to discover the term and concept of *karamarishiro* (entangling base).

自然界で、ひだは限られた体積に表面積を最大化するときに現れる。同じ原理で建築も構想できるのではないか。建築は限られた敷地に人のための表面積を最大化する営みだから。
かくして、さまざまな関係性やきっかけが内包された建築が生まれた。このアイデアは〈からまりしろ〉という言葉の発見へとつながってゆく。

ひだの幾何学は、ある種の遺伝子のように扱うこともできる。

たとえば筒のような形状の縁にひだの遺伝子を作用させると、パーマヘアみたいに広がって、上空を覆う雲のようになる。

このパビリオンはそんなアイデアを、敷き詰めると平面の中におさまらず、自然にひだができる不思議な三角形を使って実現したものだ。

The geometry of pleats can be treated as a kind of gene. If you apply a gene of pleats at the rim of a cylinder, it grows like curly hair and looks like a cloud hanging over the sky. This idea led to the creation of this pavilion with phenomenal triangles—as soon as they were placed on the grounds, they intrinsically began generating three-dimensional pleats.

I have conducted extensive research on the geometry of network-like structures, such as bubbles, and I used the geometric "gene" to create a pavilion as part of Tokyo Pavilion 2021 for the 2020 Tokyo Olympic Games. To present Japan's wooden architecture tradition and its cutting-edge technology, we used 3D cutting technology. Although our original vision of attracting people from around the world was not achieved due to the Covid-19 pandemic, the bowl did become a perfect melting pot of visitors, especially children, to "entangle themselves," as they played together in the middle of the city. Just like the flow of water vapor, or a cloud, the human flow clings around a certain shape.

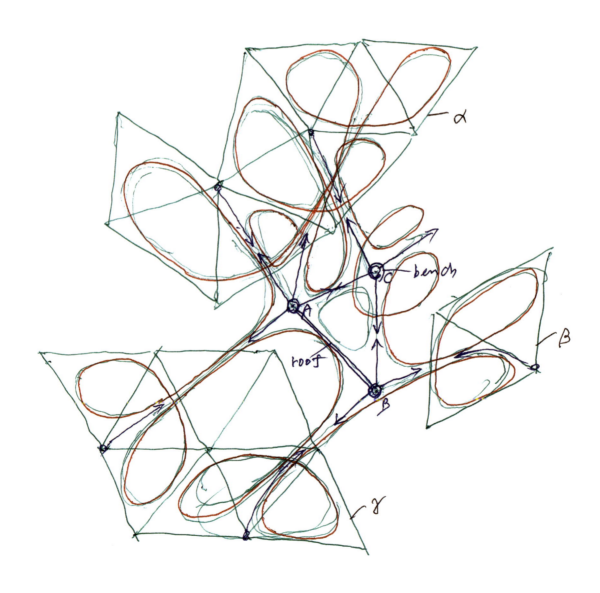

泡のようなネットワーク状の幾何学についてもいろいろと研究してきた。その遺伝子を、東京オリンピックと連動したパビリオンに用いた。

日本の木の伝統と最新テクノロジーを示すべく、木の3Dカット技術を使った。
コロナ禍の影響で、当初イメージした多国籍なてんこ盛りにはならなかったけれど、人々、とりわけ
子どもたちの絶好のからまりしろが、都市の真ん中に出現した。
人々の流れも水蒸気の流れと同様、特定の形のまわりに雲のようにまとわりつく。

台北は夥しい降水量で知られる。そんな街にできる集合住宅を、グリッドの屋根の群れで覆う。屋根の向きを4種類にし、全方面に満遍なく水が流れ、樋が溢れないようにする。

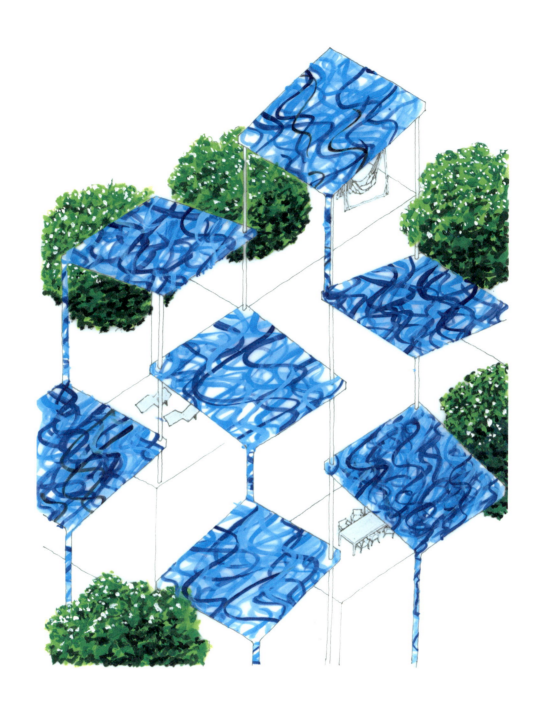

屋根は、雨水を流すためにつくられる。ある意味でそれは、水の流れに削られてできた自然の地形と同じものだ。
つまり、屋根はもう一つの自然だ。

Taipei is a city known for its heavy rainfall throughout the year. For this reason, this apartment building is covered with a grid of roofs. Roofs have been tilted in four different directions so the rainwater flows in every direction evenly and the gutters do not overflow. In a sense, the system is the same as natural topography eroded by running water. In other words, the roofs make another natural landscape. Rainwater flowing on the roofs connects people's lives inside and outside of their home, and the terraces make residents feel the presence of other residents so that they nurture a sense of a community, just as many kinds of intermediate zones in East Asia's architectural culture have connected people.

雨の化身が、内外の生活をつなぎ、湿潤な東アジアの都市的コミュニティをつなぐ。

雲も、雨も、植物たちも、人々の流れも、地形の運動も、建築をつくる人の営みも、
すべてが重層的に絡まり合っている。
〈からまりしろ〉を説明するために描いた、海藻のダイアグラムがある。魚卵が海藻に絡まり、海藻
がでこぼこした岩に絡まるとき、岩は海藻の、海藻は魚卵の、それぞれ〈からまりしろ〉である。

In and around this building, everything—the clouds, the rainwater, the plants, the flow of people, the topography and the work of people involved in the making of this building—are connected, intermingled and entangled in a multilayered manner.

To explain the concept of *karamarishiro*, a base for "entanglement," I once drew a diagram using seaweed. When fish roe are entangled with seaweed, and the seaweed is entangled with jagged rocks, the rocks make a space for the seaweed to connect, entangle and intermingle, as does the seaweed for the roe. Would it be possible to make this multilayered state into architecture? This question led me to create this building that exists in harmony with living beings, wind currents and the topographical pleats.

魚卵／海藻／岩のような重層そのものを建築にできないだろうか。
そんな問いかけはこの、さまざまな生物や風の流れ、地形のひだと共存した建築を生むことになった。

魚卵／海藻／岩の組合せは、もっと大きな建築にもなる。
たとえば小屋／土／フレームでできた台湾のデパート。

The concept inspired by the combination of fish roe, seaweed and rocks is applicable for larger architectural works. One example is this complex comprised of huts, soil and a frame.

ひだの幾何学は、大きなスケールで展開できるはずだ。台湾のシリコンバレーとも言われる新竹市中央図書館の国際コンペなら、そういう試みが受け入れられるかもしれない。

I thought that the geometry of pleats should be developed on a larger scale, and attempted to do so for the international design competition of a library in Hsinchu City, "Taiwan's Silicon Valley." Thus, the public building was designed to have a valley, created by two folded walls, as a space to display books—the knowledge. Behind walls containing stacks of every kind of book are spaces for a variety of activities based on the kind of books on the shelves. The knowledge on the shelves and activities related to it are piled up in the building, a spatialized collective unconsciousness of the people who live in the city.

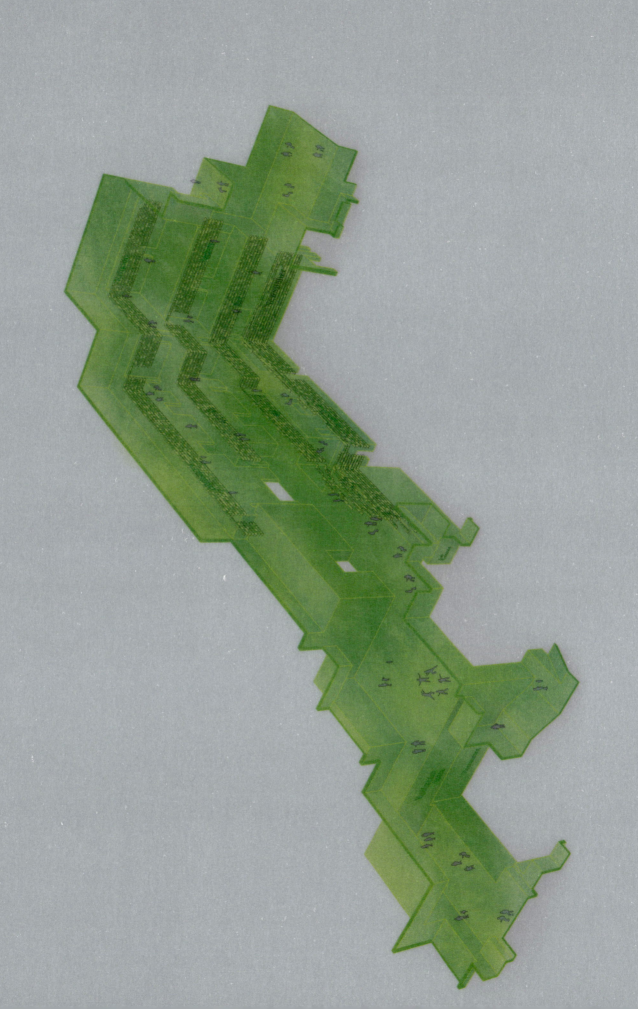

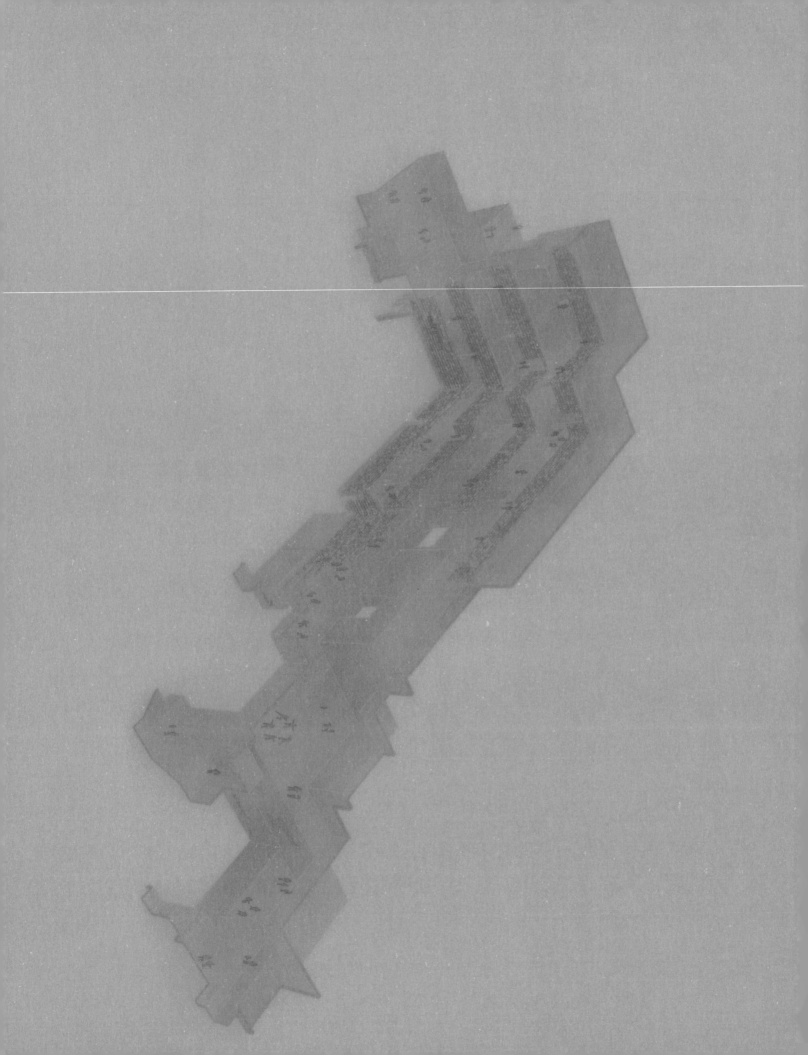

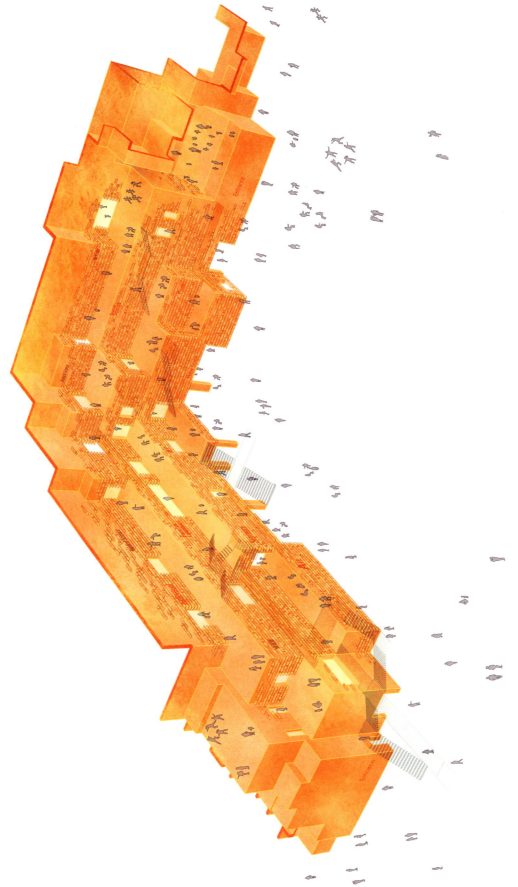

かくして、二枚のひだに挟まれた渓谷のような空間を、知のディスプレイにする公共建築が実現することになった。
あらゆる分類の本が並ぶひだの背後には、本の分類と関連したさまざまな活動の場が隣接する。
知識とその周りにある活動が集積し、市民の集合的無意識が空間化されるような場所。

知の集積といえば、市役所もさまざまな中枢的決定が行われる場である。
日本の東北エリアの中心地、仙台市役所のコンペにあたり、そんなことを考えた。

Speaking of piling up knowledge, a city hall is a place where many important decisions are made—this was the idea when I started working on the proposal for the competition of the city hall of Sendai, the heart of the Tohoku region. The 40,000m^2 open space in which office areas are spirally piled up allows divisions and departments to communicate freely and prevents a silo effect. It is a brain-like structure in which the people working there act as neurotransmitters. The pilotis under the volume offer a space to embrace communities that will help each other in times of disaster. In this tree-like hemisphere covered with plants, people move around, think and act in motion, and the collective entity begins to work in concert.

螺旋状に積層した40,000平米のワンルームは、あらゆる縦割りを横断する自由な関係を可能にする。それはさながら、さまざまな人々を情報伝達物質にした脳のようなものである。
ボリュームの下では災害時にも助け合える様々なコミュニティが育まれる。植物たちに覆われた樹のような領域の中を、人間たちが移動し、動きの中で考え、行動し、そしてそれらの総体がひとつの思考のように蠢き出す。

螺旋状に積層した40,000平米のワンルームは、あらゆる縦割りを横断する自由な関係を可能にする。
ボリュームの下では災害時にも助け合える様々なコミュニティが育まれる。

自然界では、時間の中で岩に海藻が絡まり、魚卵が絡まる。

同じように、設計の時間の中で、重層的に絡まるものたちを段階的に設計することはできないだろうか。

そうすれば、段階ごとにさまざまな人々の意見を巻き込むこともできるかもしれない。

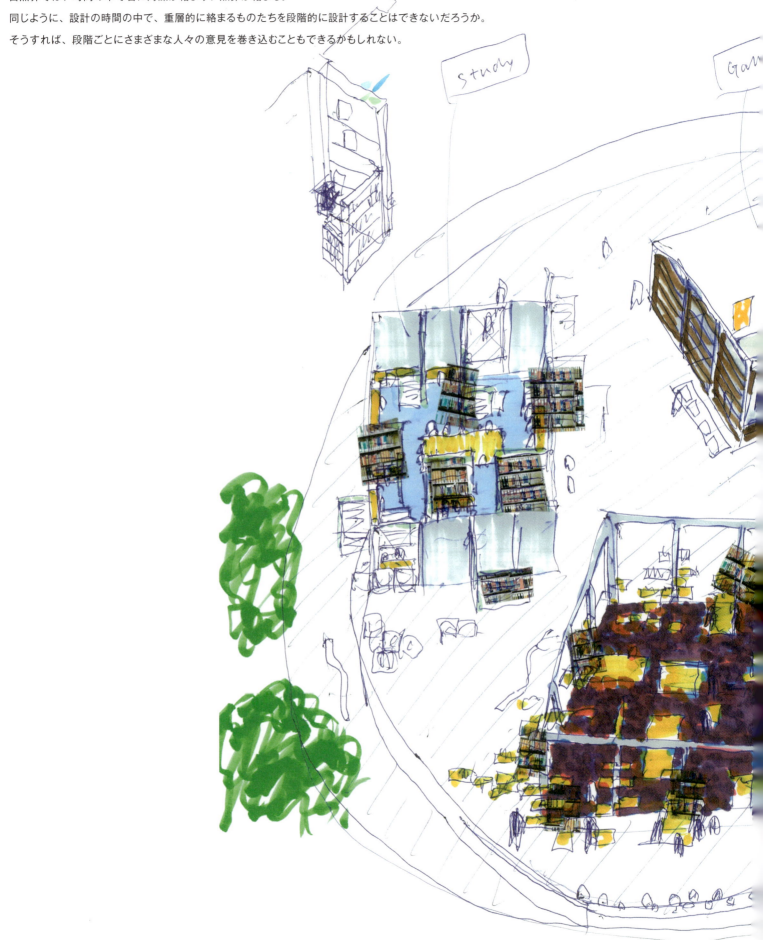

In nature, seaweed gets entangled with rocks, and fish roe with seaweed, over time. In the same way, can we design things that are entangled in a multilayered manner in the process of design, stage by stage? It might be possible to incorporate opinions of various people at each phase of development.

For the design of the Art Museum & Library, Ota public discussions were held for each of the three stages of creation: the box-like volume as a building in the city, the streets that are entangled with the volume and the built-in furniture that is entangled with the streets. As a result, numerous views and ideas, which could not be found without such a collaboration with people and businesses in Ota City, as well as numerous places that encourage people to become entangled were integrated into the building. It is just like a huge tree in the jungle, inhabited by hundreds of species.

Among the myriad perspectives during the design process, one could hear voices from the collective unconsciousness of people in Ota. A building as a base for people to become entangled—to connect, communicate and intermingle—, as well as the process to create it, is a resonance apparatus to recognize the "reverberations" of their voices.

太田市美術館・図書館の設計では、街の建物のようなボックス／その周りに絡みつくストリート／そこに絡みつく建築的家具という段階ごとにオープンな場で設計を決定することにした。その結果、太田の人々や企業と協働しないと生まれなかった無数の視点、無数のからまりしろが、ひとつの建築に凝縮された。数百種の生物が棲む、ジャングルの一本の樹のように。

設計プロセスで浮かび上がってきた無数の声は、太田の人々の集合的無意識のようなものを響かせる。
からまりしろとしての建築とプロセスは、その〈響き〉の共鳴装置だ。

街には固有の響きがある。とりわけ、整然と計画されたのではない街は、生活の分泌物のようなもので覆われ、いわば人々の無意識がつくった自然になる。

この建築のある南大塚もそんな街だ。ここに、周囲にもあるような庭付き一戸建の住宅を積層する事はできないか？

生活の場は、内部空間だけでなくその外にある庭、道路や電線や標識、向かいの庭の木々や近隣の住宅や建物たちへと開かれ、広がってゆく。

外壁は、周辺環境にある雑多な要素の色をまだらに反映した色に染まる。
南大塚の響きに新しい響きを共鳴させながら。

Every district has its own resonance. A district that was not developed in a methodological fashion is covered with the emissions of everyday life. In other words, it is a type of nature created by the unconsciousness of people living in the district.
Minami-Otsuka, where this house stands, is one of those kinds of districts. Would it be possible to design a house here by layering detached houses with gardens around it? The living space opens up and extends not only in the interior but also into the garden outside, the road, power lines, signs, trees in the garden across the street, and neighboring houses and buildings. The exterior walls are stained in mottled colors that reflect the various elements in the surrounding environment, while adding a new resonance to existing reverberations in Minami-Otsuka.

みんなが集まる広場のような場所がつくりたい、とクライアントである前橋の人々は言った。敷地を訪れて思い出したのは、輪のように広場を囲む縄文の集落だ。現代の集落はしかし、閉じた輪でなく開いた輪であって欲しい。

The client, the residents of Maebashi, said they wanted to have a plaza-like place where everyone could gather. When I visited the site, I was reminded of a Jomon settlement in which houses were arranged in a circle surrounding the plaza at the center. A modern village, however, should be a circle that opens up to the outside world, not a closed one. A green circle made of plants of apartment units floats in the air like a tree canopy. The sky framed in the middle is connected to somewhere far away. A place like a plaza for a new era was created, reverberating not only with Maebashi's cityscape, characterized by its arcades and greenery, but also with distant time and space.

住宅でできた緑の輪が樹冠のように上空に浮かぶ。真ん中の空はどこか遠くとつながっている。
アーケードや緑を特徴とした前橋の街だけでなく、遠い時空とも響き合う、新しい時代の広場のよう
な場所が生まれた。

東京屈指のファッションストリート表参道と、渋谷と原宿の街をつなぐ明治通りの交差点。都市のダイナミズムに溢れた現代の広場のようなこの場所を、さらに拡張すること。ファサードと屋上という建物の外側だけに関わる私たちのデザインは、ほぼそのことだけに捧げられている。

This building stands at the intersection of Omotesando Boulevard, one of Tokyo's most prominent fashion streets, and Meiji Avenue, which connects Shibuya and Harajuku. To further extend this place, which is like a modern-day plaza driven by urban dynamism— our endeavor to design only the exterior of the building, that is, the façade and the rooftop, was almost exclusively dedicated to this purpose. Challenging the economic requirements of the project, I carved a rooftop that slants toward the intersection wherever possible, and created a grand staircase and gardens that open up to a dynamic landscape. Here, people are thrown into the sounds and reverberations of the district, the cars, the passersby and the ever-changing sky.

経済的要求とせめぎ合いながら、可能な限り屋上を交差点に向けて削り、ダイナミックな風景に開かれた大階段と庭園をつくった。
人々はこの場所で、行き交う車や人々、刻々と変化する空や街で彩られた風景の響きの中に投げ込まれる。

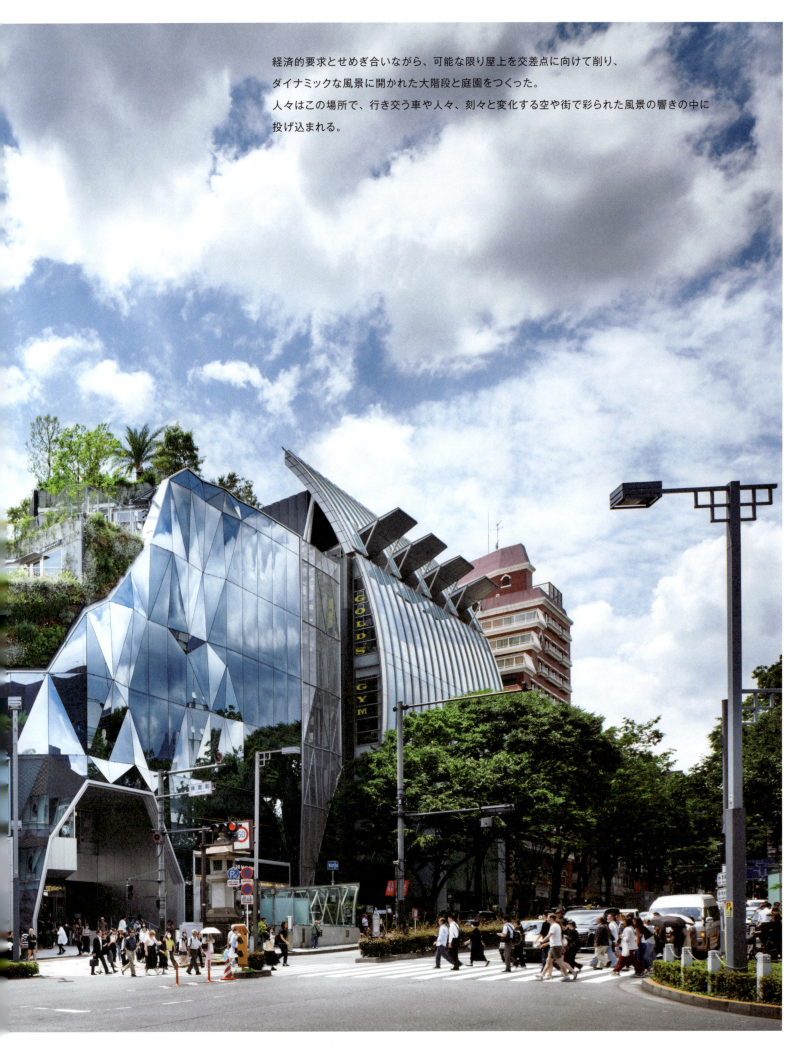

その場所の人々の思いの響きと対話して建築をつくること。
しかし、このプロジェクトまで、考えてきたのはあくまで現在を生きる人々のものでしかなかった。

数百年続くお祭りのための場所をつくるに際し、人々は明らかに自分の一生より長い時間を背負い、
あるいは自分のいない未来に向けて語っていた。

I always focused on creating architecture through dialogue with the voices of the community. Until this project, however, I was considering only people who lived in the present. In creating a place for a festival that had been passed down for hundreds of years, it was obvious that they took responsibility for a past far longer than their own lifetime, and spoke to a future time when they would no longer be alive. A procession celebrating the festival comes from somewhere across the sea, traverses hundreds of years, enters this building and goes forward to the future. Perhaps architecture was originally a place where someone else, who is not me, wandered in somewhere other than here, at a time that is not the present, and reverberated with this moment.

海の向こうのどこかからやって来たお祭りの行列は、数百年の時を超え、この建築を貫いて、
未来へと続いてゆく。

建築というものは元々、今ではないいつか、ここではないどこか、私ではない誰かが流れ込んできて、現在と響き合う場なのではなかったか。

雪深い敷地を訪れたとき、そこから越後三山が神々しく見えるのに驚いた。ここは信濃川と魚野川の合流点にあたり、魚沼に抜ける谷を介して三山が見える稀有な場所なのだ。ここには最近まで小千谷病院があり、多くの市民が同じ風景を共有している。

When I first visited the site in this snowy region, I was struck by the divine beauty of the Echigo Sanzan (the Three Mountains of Echigo). This is where the Shinano River and the Uono River merge, and it is a rare spot where the three mountains can be seen through the valley that leads to Uonuma. Until recently, Ojiya Hospital stood on the site, and most people living in the city remember the view. Artifacts from the Jomon and Paleolithic periods have been found in the area, and people thousands, or even tens of thousands, of years ago may have seen the same view. We were asked to design a complex for a local library and archives, but I think even more essential was to create a place with the quality of a sanctuary, a plaza where people can gather as they want from time to time.

I listened carefully to the reverberations that people emitted in response to their daily lives here. But there are also the reverberations emitted from time to time by the combination of mobile bookcases and books, the distant reverberations from the roofs inspired by the topography of Ojiya and the changing landscape of the three mountains. What kind of reverberations of reverberations will be created between the different phases?

地域からは縄文や旧石器時代の遺物も見つかっており、数千年前、ことによれば数万年前の人々も同じ風景を見ていたかもしれない。

私たちに直接求められているのは図書館と資料館の設計なのだが、より本質的に求められているのは、ある種の聖地性を持ち、事あるごとに人々が集まれる広場のような場所なのではないか。

もちろんここでの日常に対して人々が発する〈響き〉には丁寧に耳を傾けた。
しかしここではさらに、移動式の書架と資料の組合せが時々に発する〈響き〉、小千谷の地形に触発された屋根や三山の移り変わる風景が引き寄せる遠い〈響き〉が折り重なる。
位相の異なるこれらの間にどんな〈響きの響き〉が生まれるだろうか。

A friend of mine from architecture school days, who has taken over the family business in Matsue City, Shimane Prefecture, asked me to design a house for him. We have visited many architectural works together and share the same taste for films, music, books and other contemporary arts and cultures. However, I knew very little about him as a Matsue native. The site, by Matsue Castle, is surrounded by trees that remind of the taste of the previous owner, who was a tea master. Just a stone's throw away is Meimeian, a masterpiece tea pavilion by Matsudaira Fumai, a feudal lord and tea master of the Edo period. And needless to say, this region is home to Izumo mythology.

My friend has an affection for modern and contemporary designs, and lives and works in a city rich in history and culture. Though these attributes may seem to be in opposition, I think they coexist and resonate without contradiction. I wanted to create an architecture that embodies this reality.

The key to this project is the thick roof that looks somehow light. The roof links his affection for modern, industrial designs to the thick, stout forms found in traditional designs in Matsue—the thatched roof of the Meimeian tea pavilion, the Izumo Nankin goldfish favored by Fumai, the huge Shinto straw rope of Izumo Taisha Grand Shrine. Trees are seen and felt in between the fragmented roofs, and their existence echoes in the space.

Contemporary reverberations, reverberations from the city of Matsue, and reverberations from the garden. Reverberations from different phases of the place overlap to create reverberations of reverberations.

松江で家業を継いだ建築学科時代の友人が、自宅を設計しろという。彼とは多くの建築を見て歩いたし、映画や音楽、本の好みなど現代性の部分は概ね共有している。とはいえ松江人としての彼のことはほとんど知らない。

松江城そばの敷地は、茶人だったという先住者の趣味が偲ばれる樹木に囲まれている。目と鼻の先には江戸時代の大名茶人、松平不昧による『明明庵』もある。そしてここは出雲神話の地でもある。

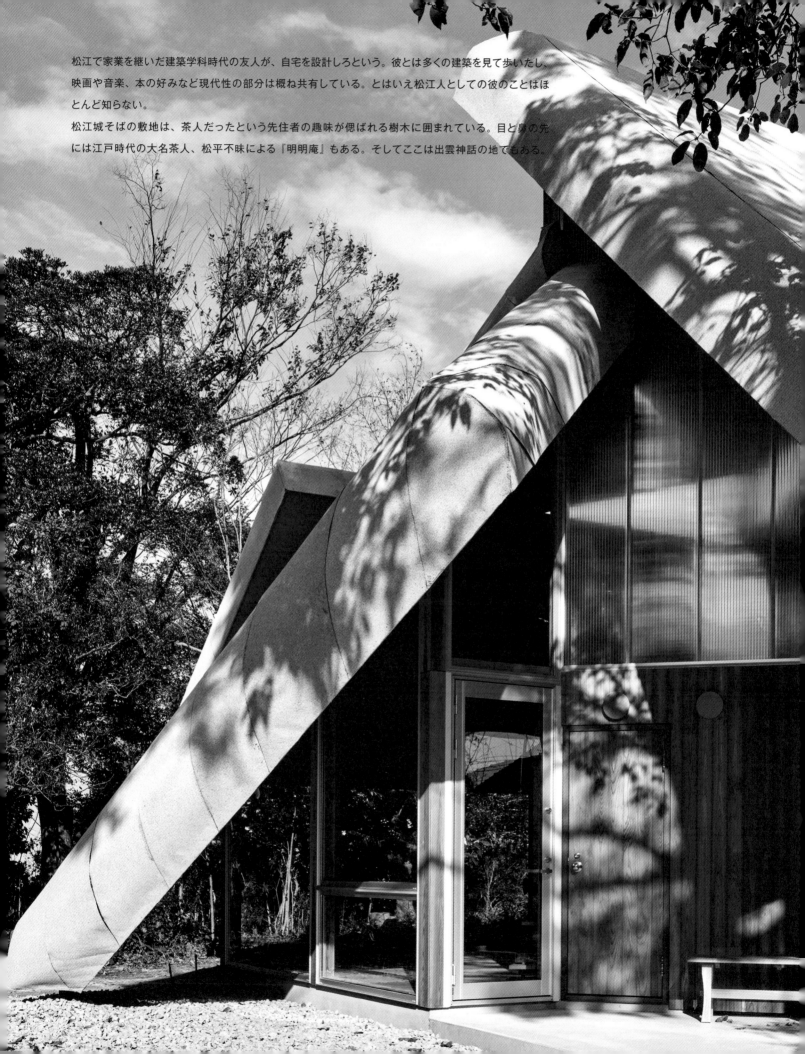

現代的デザインへの志向と松江の中でのさまざまな文化や関係性。対立するようだが、彼の中では予盾なく共存し、響き合っているだろう。そういうリアリティをそのまま建築にしたいと思った。

ここでは分厚いがどことなく軽い屋根が鍵である。これを結び目として現代的でインダストリアルな感覚と、松江のぼってりした造形感覚（『明明庵』の茅葺、不昧好みの金魚『出雲なんきん』、出雲大社の標縄…）が響き合う。断片化した屋根の間から庭の樹木の感覚が流れ込み、響き合う。

現代の響き、松江の響き、庭の響き。異なる位相の響きが重なり、〈響きの響き〉が生まれる。

山形市民会館の提案を地元の人々と一緒に行った。
閉じた箱ではなく、普段から市民が集まり、観光客も惹きよせられるような、
からまりしろとしてのホールは可能か。

たどり着いたのは様々な突出部を持つホールの形式をさらに分岐させた、大樹のような建築だった。

木の塊から彫り出されたかのような羽黒山五重塔や、岩を穿ってつくられた山寺に象徴されるような、
山形の精神性を引き寄せる場が、創造的な市民活動をはぐくむ。

I created a proposal for the Yamagata Civic Hall in collaboration with the local community. Would it be possible to create a hall that is not a closed box, but rather a place where citizens could gather on a regular basis and that would attract tourists, a place for people to intermingle? In the end, what we arrived was architecture like a big tree—the typical form of a hall with many protrusions was developed further with portions branched out. Just like the five-story pagoda of Mt. Haguro, which looks as if it has been carved from a block of wood, and the Yamadera temple, which looks as if it was carved out of a rock, the structure offers a place that epitomizes the spirituality of Yamagata and will foster creative civic activities.

雲のような巨大な閲覧空間が、ランドスケープと連続した市民活動の場所の上に浮かぶ。
浮かぶのは省エネルギーや本の日焼けを考慮して、開口率をギリギリまで抑えた高断熱で希薄な箱。
しかし無数に開けられた小さな開口によって、内部に木漏れ日のような光が差し込む。

A huge, cloud-like reading room is placed above the space extending from the landscape for communal activities. To improve energy conservation and protect books from sun damage, the room is contained in a super-insulated box made of thin materials with a minimum aperture ratio. Through countless tiny openings, however, daylight filters into the interior, like dappled sunlight through the leaves. The openings are plotted in consideration of the movement of the sun through the year, and daylight reaches the first floor through the void at the structure's center. This library is a place to connect with the "distance," by accessing the vast amount of knowledge in books and, at the same time, feeling the movement of celestial bodies through the shifting daylight.

2025年に予定されている大阪・関西万博に、古代から国際交流のゲートであり続けた大阪の海や大地との関係をセレブレートする、生命のような建築をつくろうとしている。複数の帯が織りなす空気をまとった屋外の広がりと、屋内の催事の場が入り混じる、生き生きとした環境を目指した。

For the Expo 2025 Osaka, Kansai, Japan, we are creating a lifelike architecture that will celebrate the relationship between the sea and the land of Osaka, a place that has been a gateway for international exchange since ancient times. A lively environment is created by blurring the borders of the expansive outdoor space in multiple *obi* sash-like sections and the event spaces in the interior. The obi-like sections are placed diagonal to the shape of the site, but in parallel with the fold in the geography of the Kansai region that runs from the southwest to the northeast, as well as the direction of the steady winds that flow over the Yodo River. Reverberating with the earth as a geographic organism, the architecture clad in the energy of wind, water, and light will be remembered in the future.

敷地に対して斜めにかしいだ帯の方向は、関西を斜めに貫く地形のしわと同期し、淀川水系へと抜ける定常風の方向と一致している。

ジオグラフィックな生命体としての地球と響き合う建築は、風や水、光のエネルギーをまとった、未来の記憶となるだろう。

これからの100年におけるUniversityにふさわしい、
台湾大学100年を記念する場の国際コンペに勝った。
博物館、多目的ホール、宿泊施設などからなるコンプレックスである。

私たちは、中核をなす博物館がレクチャルームやオーディトリアムなどと融合し、展示と対話、パフォーマンスが絡まり合う「NEW FORUM」となることを提案した。

We won the international competition for a project to commemorate the centenary of National Taiwan University. The complex includes a museum, a multipurpose hall (auditorium) and accommodation facilities. In our proposal, the museum, the core of the complex, is integrated with lecture rooms and the auditorium to create a new forum where exhibitions, discussions and performances are intertwined. Specifically, by arranging "Stripes," the platforms for activities, as five-line staffs, and "Figures," exhibition spaces with unique characters for each field, as musical notes on them, a variety of functions are connected and disconnected, creating a place of resonances.

具体的には、五線譜のようなStripe（プラットフォーム状の場）と音符のようなFigure（分野ごとの特徴ある展示空間）の組合せによって、さまざまな機能が結びついたり離れたりする響き合いの場が生まれる。

In response to the challenge of designing a new public building that would connect art, books, people, and the local community of Nukui, we set the goal of "creating a *fujizuka* for the 21st century."

A fujizuka is a manmade mound from which to enjoy the view of Mt. Fuji from a distance, and many were built in the Edo period (1603-1867) to resemble Mt. Fuji. Combining a view of a distant Mt. Fuji with a view of the fictional Fuji mound in the foreground, they evoke a virtual reality-like imagination that is also expressed in contemporary art pieces as well as in anime, a treasured creative industry of Nerima Ward. We therefore sought to create reverberations between people's memories with the place for art and books by designing a hill-like building that people can climb—a modern-day fujizuka. The connection between the extraordinariness of Mt. Fuji with the everydayness of the building will create reverberations of reverberations unique to this place.

This project reflects almost everything I have been thinking about "entanglement" and "resonance." The building contains a multilayer structure constructed of interconnected elements—which we named Shelters, Shelves and Shades—to protect and preserve precious art pieces and books. Shelters are functional boxes such as galleries and storage rooms, and we designed Shelves and Shades integrated with Shelters through a series of workshops to hear and understand the voices of the local people of Nerima. This is not only about the design process. In particular, creative activities by the local community will always unfold around Shelves, and their lively communal voices will magnificently reverberate.

アートと本、人々、貫井の街をつなぐ新しい公共建築という課題を受けて、私たちが掲げたのは「21世紀の富士塚をつくる」というものだった。

富士塚とは、富士山を遠くから見るために江戸時代に生まれた富士に似せた人工の丘のことで、練馬区にも幾つかの富士塚がある。遠方に望む富士山と近景のフィクショナルな富士塚という設定は、現代アートや練馬の宝であるアニメーションとも通じる仮想現実的な想像力を喚起する。

そこで私たちは、現代の富士塚のような、人々が登ることのできる丘状の建築によって、人々の記憶とアートや本の場とを響き合わせようとしたのだ。日常的用途とは異なる位相にある富士山とのつながりが、ここにしかない〈響きの響き〉、日常と非日常の響き合いをつくり出すだろう。

このプロジェクトには、〈からまり〉や〈響き〉についてこれまで思考してきたことの、ほとんどすべてが反映されている。

この建築は大切な美術品や本を守る多重構造=Shelter/Shelf/Shadeを持つ。Shelterは展示室や収蔵庫などの機能的な箱だが、それを囲むShelfやShadeに関しては、練馬の人々が発する〈響き〉と対話しながら設計するために、ワークショップを重ねてきた。

プロセスだけの話ではない。特にShelfは、いつ行ってもさまざまな創造的市民活動が展開する、壮大な生きた〈響き〉のディスプレイとなるだろう。

My concept of "entangling" is also fully developed throughout the building. Visitors will experience a comfortable cohesiveness as they walk by and get inspired by books and art. This complex will also be a place for inclusion, where everybody can enjoy a three-dimensional space that awakens their untamed creativity and imagination.
"Entangling," "reverberating," and "reverberations of reverberations."
We hope that, as individuals, architects can create such a circuit through these concepts, and explore the architecture of a new era by embracing fundamental changes in humanity.
We also hope that through such architecture, diverse joy can be shared by many people.
We are creating architecture toward such hopes.

また〈からまりしろ〉をめぐる思考は各所に生かされている。ここを訪れる人は自分の身体を使って本やアートを感じる、居心地の良い様々なまとまりを体験するだろう。また、動物的本能を呼び覚ますような、立体的な空間の喜びを、身体的条件に関わりなくすべての人々が感じられる場所になるだろう。

〈からまりしろ〉、〈響き〉、〈響きの響き〉…。
個としての建築家が、そんな回路を通して「人間」の根本的な変容を受け止め、新しい時代の建築を切り拓くことができるなら。また、そのような建築を通して、多様な喜びのようなものが、多くの人々に共有されるなら。
そんな希望に向けて、僕たちは建築をつくっている。

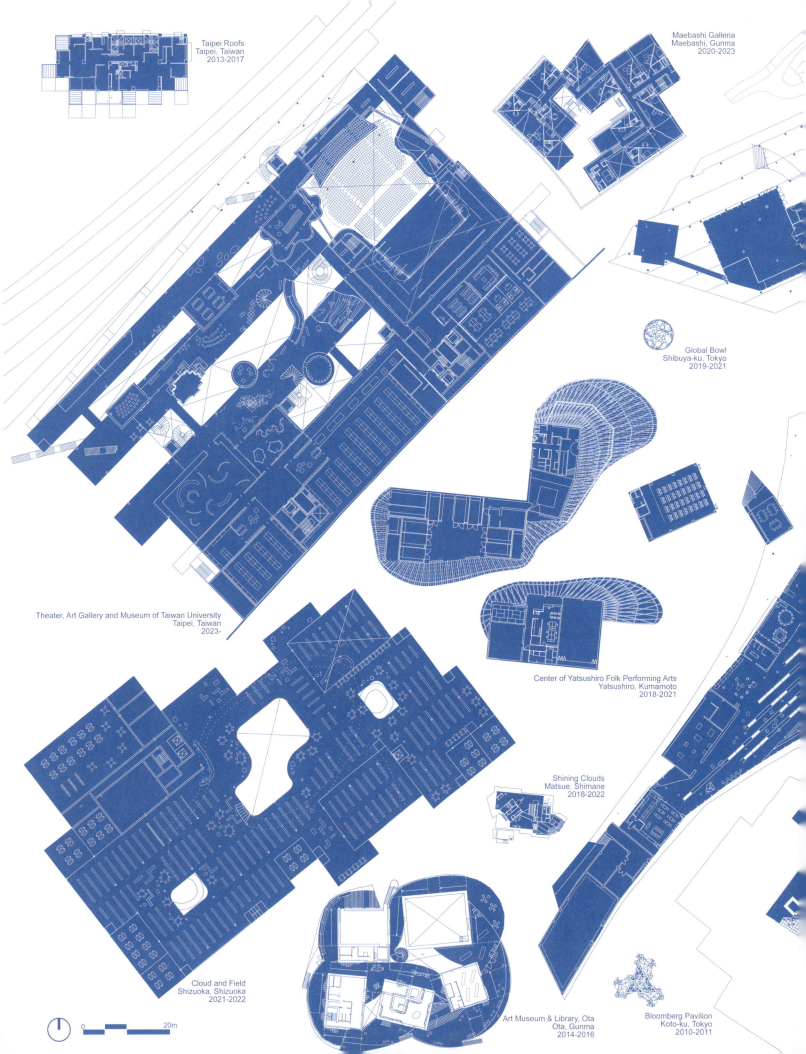

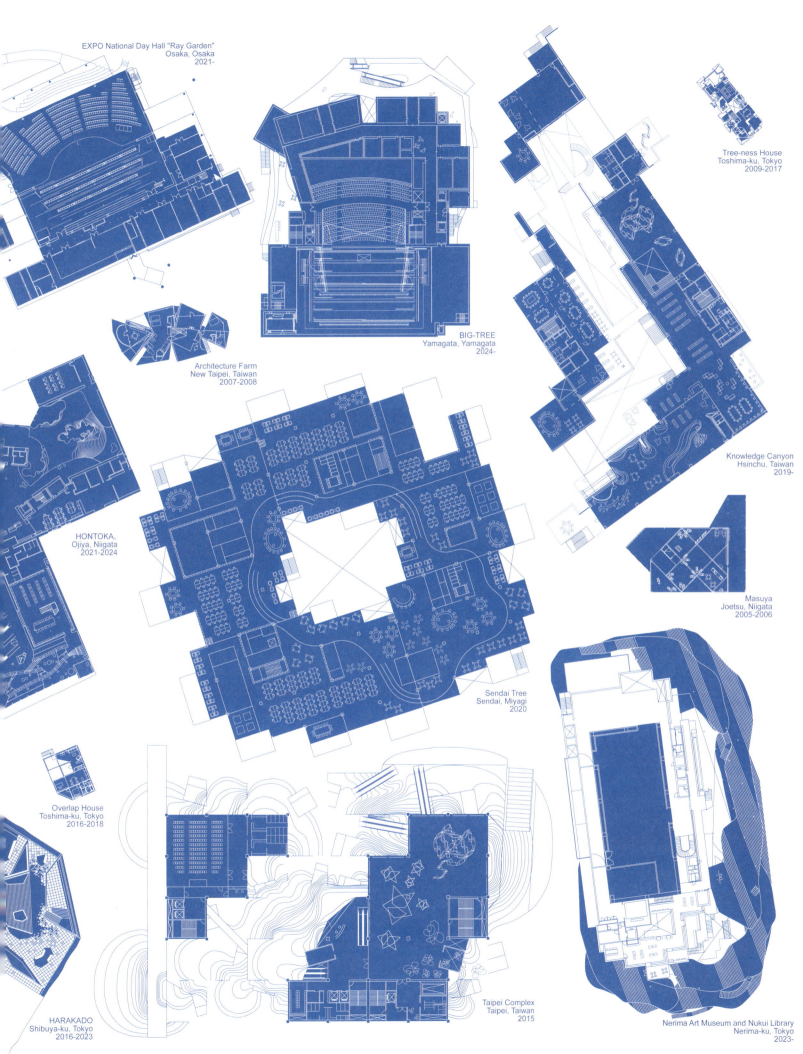

解説・概要データ
Explanation and Data

掲載ページ　pp.
作品名｜Title (proposal／unbuild／progress)
解説｜explanation

所在地｜location
主要用途｜principal use
設計期間｜design period
施工期間｜construction period
構造｜structure
建築面積｜building area
延床面積｜total floor area
規模｜number of stories

---

pp.16-19
桝屋本店
Masuya

新潟県に建つ小型農機具のためのショールーム。5mグリッド
で配置したコンクリート壁を、平面的に45度振り、さらに斜め
にカットする。人の動きとともに移ろいゆく自然環境のような、
人間の動物的な部分に訴えかける一体空間である。
This showroom for small agricultural machinery is
located in Niigata. The design features concrete walls,
arrayed in a 5m grid, that are tilted at a 45-degree
angle and cut diagonally. This creates a unified space
that taps into the primal aspects of human nature,
reminiscent of the dynamic natural environment that
changes as one navigates through it.

新潟県上越市｜Joetsu, Niigata
ショールーム、事務所｜showroom, office
May 2005－November 2005
April 2006－September 2006
Reinforced concrete
294m^2
213m^2
2 stories

---

pp.20-23
Architecture Farm
（unbuild）

台湾北部の自然に囲まれた丘に建つ住宅。複雑なプログラム
をパブリックとプライベートに二分する一つの表面を考え、そ
れをひだ化させることで、それぞれの領域が互いに繋がってい
るが見通せない、複雑な距離を内包した連続的な空間をつくり
だした。
This residence on a hill in northern Taiwan is
enveloped by nature. It treats a complex layout as a
single surface to be divided into public and private
spaces. The design incorporates folds to form a
continuous yet intricately distanced space, allowing
connectivity without visibility.

台湾 新北｜New Taipei, Taiwan
住宅｜house
November 2007－June 2008
－
Reinforced concrete + Steel flame
253m^2
495m^2
3 stories

---

pp.24-27
Bloomberg Pavilion

東京都現代美術館に建てられた小さなパビリオン。ハイプレイ
ンと呼ばれる幾何学によって、同じ形の反復で複雑なひだが生
成される。1.6mmの鉄板でつくられたひだは日射を遮り、室内
に柔らかい光をもたらす雲のようなリフレクターになる。
This small pavilion at the Museum of Contemporary
Art Tokyo has combines geometric shapes in what is
called a hyplane structure, producing a continuous
curved, pleated surface. Constructed from 1.6mm
thick steel sheets, the pleats are reflectors that serve
like clouds, blocking direct sunlight and diffusing soft
light within the space.

東京都江東区｜Koto-ku, Tokyo
パビリオン｜pavilion
May 2010－April 2011
May 2011－October 2011
Steel flame
25m^2
1 story

---

pp.28-31
Global Bowl

東京オリンピックに際して国連大学前の広場に建設したパビ
リオン。孔だらけのボウルは、内外の境界をほどきつつ結ぶ、
反転する幾何学でできており、都市の中に小さな閉域をつくり
ながら、同時に外側とつながる。木材を3次元カットして組み
合わせる、日本の伝統と最新技術を生かした建築である。
Constructed in the plaza of United Nations University
for the Tokyo Olympics, this pavilion features a design
with a porous bowl structure, using inverted geometry
to dissolve and traverse boundaries between inside
and outside, creating a small enclosed space within
the city while maintaining a connection with the
exterior. The structure combines Japanese traditional
techniques with state-of-the-art technology through
3D cutting and assembling of wood.

東京都渋谷区｜Shibuya-ku, Tokyo
パビリオン｜pavilion
January 2019－May 2021
June 2021－June 2021
Wooden
－
36.4m^2
1 story

---

pp.32-37
富富話合
Taipei Roofs

台北に建つ地上12階建ての集合住宅。セットバックによって、
すべての住戸が大きなテラスを持てるようにした。テラスは屋
根や樹木で覆われ、建物表面に立体的で快適な中間領域がで
きる。水や空気の流れが絡まる、21世紀のアジアにふさわし
い高層建築のプロトタイプである。
This 12-story apartment house in Taipei is strategically
designed with setbacks, ensuring that each unit has a
spacious terrace. The terraces, covered with roofs and
trees, form a pleasant three-dimensional space on the
building's exterior. Designed to incorporate flows of
water and air, this structure serves as a prototype for
21st-century high-rise architecture in Asia.

台湾 台北｜Taipei, Taiwan
物販店舗・共同住宅｜commercial facility, apartment house
February 2013－March 2014
April 2014－October 2017
Reinforced concrete + Steel flame
508.5m^2
3,364m^2
15 stories, 3 basements

---

pp.38-43
Tree-ness House

東京に建つ住宅とギャラリーの複合ビル。一本の樹が幹／枝
／葉からなるように、箱／ひだ／植物を有機的に組合わせた建
築である。建物の内部空間だけを立体化するのではなく、庭
や道のような外部空間も含めた全体を三次元化している。
Located in Tokyo, Tree-ness House combines residential
and gallery spaces. Like the natural structure of a
tree with a trunk, branches, and leaves, the building
organically combines boxes, folds, and vegetation.
Not only the interior, but also external spaces like the
garden and the street, are incorporated into an overall
three-dimensional whole.

東京都豊島区｜Toshima-ku, Tokyo
ギャラリー・共同住宅｜gallery, apartment house
December 2009－September 2015
December 2015－August 2017
Reinforced concrete
99.68m^2
450m^2
5 stories

---

pp.44-45
Taipei Complex
（unbuild）

台北に建つ美術館・店舗・レストランからなる複合施設。RC
ラーメン構造のフレーム／土と植物／集落のようなパビリオン
という互いに違和感のある要素を階層的に共存させる。結果と
して、建物と土と人々のアクティビティーが渾然一体に混ざり
合う、未来の集落ともいうべき光景が生まれるだろう。
This mixed-use facility in Taipei City houses a
museum, shops, and restaurants. It uniquely combines
disparate elements, including a reinforced concrete
(RC) rigid-structured frame, soil, plants, and pavilions
reminiscent of small villages. This design will produce
a futuristic village atmosphere where architecture,
nature, and human activity seamlessly intertwine.

台湾 台北｜Taipei, Taiwan
美術館、店舗、レストラン複合施設｜museum, shops,
restaurants
April 2015－
－
Reinforced concrete + Steel flame
3,806m^2
27,000m^2
7 stories, 3 basements

---

pp.46-49
新竹市中央図書館　※1
Knowledge Canyon （progress）

台湾新竹の中央図書館。街の文化ゾーンをつなぐグリーンベ
ルトに沿った二枚の知識の壁が、さまざまな場所をはらみなが

らひだをなし、その間に渓谷のようなリーディングルームができる。あらゆる分類の本が並ぶこの壁の背後には、本の内容と関連した活動の場を設ける。本とコミュニケーションが融合した拡張された図書館である。

This is a design for the central library in Hsinchu City, Taiwan, located on a green belt that links the city's cultural zone. The library features two "walls of knowledge" forming complex folds that define various spaces, with a canyon-like reading room nestled between them. Behind the walls, filled with books across all genres, are spaces for activities linked to the content of the books, fostering an expanded library environment where literature and communication merge.

台湾 新竹｜Hsinchu, Taiwan
図書館、オフィス｜library, office
September 2019 − March 2020
June 2020 −
Reinforced concrete ＋ Steel flame
8,460.22m²
30,919.26m²
4 stories, 2 basements

---

pp.50-53
Sendai Tree ※2
(proposal)

仙台市役所本庁舎建替のプロポーザル案。螺旋を成す40,000m²のワンルーム（オフィス）による〈樹〉と、街と地続きに連続し市民活動の拠点となる〈丘〉から構成される。人々と共にそだてる、緑に覆われた一本の巨樹のような市役所である。

This proposal for the new Sendai City Hall features a 40,000 m² single-room (office) in the form of a "tree" spiraling upward, mimicking a tree, combined with a "hill" that blends into the urban landscape, serving as a base for civic activities. Enveloped in greenery, the city hall is designed to grow alongside the community like a giant tree.

宮城県仙台市｜Sendai, Miyagi
庁舎｜city hall
August 2020 − Decemger 2020
−
Reinforced concrete ＋ Steel flame
7,241.8m²
58,810m²
15 stories, 3 basements

---

pp.54-63
太田市美術館・図書館
Art Museum & Library, Ota

群馬県太田駅前に建つ文化交流施設。5つのRC造の「ボックス」の周りに鉄骨造の「リム」によるスロープが取り巻く、街が内部まで連続しているような建築である。閑散とした駅前に人の流れを取り戻すための拠点にふさわしく、多数の市民や関係者を巻き込みつつ設計した。

Situated in front of Ota Station in Gunma Prefecture, this cultural exchange facility consists of five reinforced concrete (RC) "boxes" encircled by a steel "rim" of slopes, giving the impression that the city extends into the building. It was designed with the involvement of numerous citizens and stakeholders, fittingly for a project that aims to revitalize the deserted area around the station.

群馬県太田市｜Ota, Gunma
図書館、美術館｜library, museum
April 2014 − March 2015
May 2015 − December 2016
Reinforced concrete ＋ Steel flame
1,496.87m²
3,150m²
3 stories, 1 basement

---

pp.64-69
Overlap House

東京都南大塚に建つ3つの庭付一戸建てが積層したような集合住宅。周辺の街の中にある何気ない色合いを擬態のように反映したスレートのまだらなパターンで屋根と壁を覆った。周辺の地形と連続するようなボリュームと相まって、南大塚の街の響きを反映しつつ、更新している。

Located in Minamiotsuka, Tokyo, this apartment house is designed to resemble stacked single-family homes with gardens. The roofs and walls are clad in a mottled slate pattern, reflecting the subdued hues of the surrounding urban environment and blending the structure's volume with the local topography, and revitalizing the atmosphere of Minamiotsuka while reflecting its resonance.

東京都豊島区｜Toshima-ku, Tokyo
共同住宅｜apartment house
May 2016 − June 2017
July 2017 − May 2018
Steel flame
87.9m²
190.62m²
3 stories

---

pp.70-73
まえばしガレリア
Maebashi Galleria

集合住宅、ギャラリー、レストランからなる複合施設。前橋に関わる様々な人たちと議論を重ねて計画がされたのは一本の樹のような建築だった。輪をなす住居群を、壁面緑化を施すことで樹冠さながら空中に浮かべ、その下に店舗と中庭が一体化した広場をつくっている。

This mixed-use facility in Maebashi comprises residential units, a gallery, and restaurants. Developed after extensive consultations with local stakeholders, it features a tree-like design with a circular arrangement of residences elevated like a tree canopy, integrated with vertical greening. Below this array, shops and a courtyard merge to form a public plaza.

群馬県前橋市｜Maebashi, Gunma
共同住宅、商業施設｜apartment house, comercial facility
January 2020 − December 2021
January 2022 − May 2023
Steel flame
1,831.65m²
3,269.05m²
4 stories

---

pp.74-77
HARAKADO

表参道と明治通り交差点に計画された商業施設。そのファサードと屋上のデザインを行った。ファサードは「まちを編む」とい

うコンセプトで、緑と街を映しだす反射質のガラスを多角形の織物のように巡らせた。屋上にはダイナミックな風景に開かれた大階段と庭園をつくり、立体的に拡張された交差点をつくった。

This is a design for the facade and rooftop of a commercial facility planned for the intersection of Omotesando and Meiji-dori. With the concept of "weaving the city," the facade is covered with reflective glass in a pattern akin to multifaceted textiles, which mirrors the greenery and urban surroundings. The rooftop features a grand staircase and a garden, offering dynamic views and creating a three-dimensional extension of the intersection.

東京都渋谷区｜Shibuya-ku, Tokyo
商業施設｜comercial facility
February 2016 − Nobember 2020
December 2020 − August 2023
Reinforced concrete ＋ Steel flame
2,357.99m²
19,893.74m²
9 stories, 3 basements

---

pp.78-87
八代市民俗伝統芸能伝承館
Center of Yatsushiro Folk Performing Arts

熊本県に建つ民俗伝統芸能関連の品を展示・保存し、お祭りの踊りを練習する場も備えた複合施設。八代妙見祭の笠鉾のような伝統的な木組や曲線を取り入れ、八代産製材の3Dプレカットによって織物のような構成をもった三次元曲面の屋根をつくっている。現代的な技術を生かして伝統を感じさせる木造建築を実現している。

Located in Kumamoto, this facility serves as a space for display and preservation of items associated with folk performing arts, and as a venue for practicing festival dances. It incorporates traditional timber structure and curves that echo the Yatsushiro Myoken Festival's floats, and has a complex curved roof, made from Yatsushiro timber pre-cut in a 3D structure, that evokes a textile. The building combines contemporary technology with traditional design in a wooden structure that resonates with history.

熊本県八代市｜Yatsushiro, Kumamoto
博物館｜museum
July 2018 − September 2019
October 2019 − June 2021
Reinforced concrete ＋ Wooden
1,907.39m²
1,722.74m²
2 stories

---

pp.88-95
ホントカ。小千谷市ひと・まち・文化共創拠点
HONTOKA. Ojiya City People, Town, Cultural Co-creation Base

新潟県に建つ図書館を中心とした複合施設。資料のさまざまな組み合わせを可能にする移動式の書架〈Float〉／市民活動の場となる個性あるへや〈Anchor〉／越後三山や小千谷縮、錦鯉の群れ、信濃川の流れを思わせる〈Roof〉という三つの要素で構成されている。遠い昔の記憶、小千谷の伝統、市民の日常を結びつける建築である。

The mixed-use facility in Niigata Prefecture revolves around a library and incorporates three key elements: movable bookshelves "Floats", unique rooms "Anchors" for community activities, and a "Roof" that evokes the Echigo Mountains, Ojiya-chijimi fabric, schools of Nishiki-goi carp, and the flow of the Shinano River. The structure links distant memories, the traditions of Ojiya, and the everyday lives of its citizens.

新潟県小千谷市｜Ojiya, Niigata
図書館、複合施設｜library complex
April 2021－June 2022
November 2022－September 2024
Reinforced concrete ＋ Steel flame
4,283.22m²
4,631.04m²
2 stories

---

pp.96-101
シャイニング・クラウズ
Shining Clouds

島根県松江市に建つ個人住宅。庭を造るように、二つのコアを据え、そのまわりに生活の設えを配した上に、九つに断片化した分厚い屋根を浮かべた。重くも軽くも、和でも洋でもない、多様で曖昧な様相を持ち、あらゆるものと響き合うような住宅である。
This private residence in Matsue City, Shimane Prefecture, is designed as if sculpting a garden, with two cores around which living spaces are organized, capped with a thick roof fragmented into nine parts. The home has a diverse and ambiguous character that is neither distinctly Japanese nor Western, neither heavy nor light, and resonates with everything in its surroundings.

島根県松江市｜Matsue, Shimane
住宅｜house
October 2018－November 2021
January 2022－November 2022
Wooden
104.89m²
120.25m²
2 stories

---

pp.102-107
BIG-TREE ※3
（progress）

市民や観光客がひきよせられる一本の巨樹のような市民会館。フライタワーを幹とし、客席や楽屋等を枝のように派生させることで巨大な劇場のボリュームが分節され、様々な市民活動が絡み合う場所が生まれる。山や樹々と共に過ごしてきた山形の精神性をシンボライズする建築である。
This civic hall in Yamagata resembles a giant tree, welcoming locals and tourists alike. With a fly loft (theatrical rigging system) as the trunk and the seating and backstage areas arrayed like branches, the enormous volume of the theater space is segmented, creating interconnected spaces for various community activities. This structure is symbolic of Yamagata's spirit and informed by its history of coexistence with mountains and trees.

山形県山形市｜Yamagata, Yamagata
コンサートホール｜concert hall
August 2024－
－
Reinforced concrete ＋ Steel flame
2,830m²
11,440m²
10 stories, 2 basements

---

pp.108-111
Cloud and Field
（proposal）

静岡県立中央図書館コンペ案。四角い箱を重ね合わせた「雲」＝〈CLOUD〉を空中に浮かべ、知の集蔵体とすると同時に、その下に情報と自然が入り混じるランドスケープ＝〈FIELD〉をつくる。太陽の軌道に沿った無数の小さな開口からさしこむ光を通して、自然の大きな拡がりを感じられるようになっている。
A competition proposal for the Shizuoka Prefectural Central Library, this design layers rectangular boxes to create a "Cloud," suspended above as a repository of knowledge, while a "Field" below integrates information with the natural environment. The project features numerous small apertures aligned with the sun's trajectory, allowing light to filter through and giving visitors the sense of a vast natural expanse.

静岡県静岡市｜Shizuoka, Shizuoka
図書館｜library
October 2021－February 2022
－
Steel flame
6,333.9m²
19,600m²
8 stories

---

pp.112-115
EXPO ナショナルデーホール「レイガーデン」 ※2
EXPO National Day Hall "Ray Garden" （progress）

2025年日本国際博覧会において、多数の機能（催事場、ラウンジ・ダイニング、展示場、小ステージ）を担う催事用の複合施設。光や風、緑を含んだ複数の帯状のスラブからなる。定常風に対応した帯の方向は、関西の地形のしわの方向と一致し、ジオグラフィックな生命体としての地球の活動を照らしだしている。
This mixed-use facility for EXPO 2025 includes an event space, lounge dining, an exhibition area, and a small stage. The design features multiple stripe-like slabs that integrate light, wind, and greenery. The orientation of the slabs is strategically aligned with the prevailing winds and the topographical folds of the Kansai region, thereby reflecting the geological activity of the Earth as a living organism.

大阪府大阪市｜Osaka, Osaka
ホール、展示場、ラウンジ｜hall, gallery, lounge
November 2021－October 2023
December 2023－
Steel flame
3,526.74m²
4,836.97m²
2 stories

---

pp.116-121
臺灣大學 藝文大樓 ※4
Theater, Art Gallery and Museum of Taiwan University
（progress）

台湾大学創立百周年を記念する、博物館、多目的ホール、宿泊施設等からなる複合施設。これからの100年を見据えて、展示と対話、パフォーマンスがからまり合う「NEW FORUM」を提案した。五線譜のようなStripe（プラットフォーム状の場）と音符のようなFigure（分野ごとの特徴ある展示空間）の組合せによって、様々な機能が結びついたり離れたりする響き合いの場が生まれる。Figureによって安定した個々の展示空間をつくりながら、Figureを一望することによって台湾大学の学術交流が可視化される。
This is a proposal for a complex celebrating the centennial of National Taiwan University, featuring a museum, a multipurpose hall, accommodations and more. It incorporates a "New Forum" where exhibitions, discussions, and performances can be synergistically held. The architectural design includes a Stripe (platform-like space) resembling a musical staff, and musical note-like Figures (distinct spaces for each field), creating a dynamic space where various functions converge and diverge. The Figures serve as separate, stable exhibition spaces, fostering a visual representation of academic exchange at the university.

台湾 台北｜Taipei, Taiwan
博物館、美術館、劇場、宿泊施設、オフィス｜museum, art gallery, theater, accomodation, office
January 2023－
－
Reinforced concrete ＋ Steel flame
－
55,378m²
12 stories, 3 basements

---

pp.122-131
練馬区立美術館・貫井図書館
Nerima Art Museum and Nukui Library （progress）

練馬区立美術館・貫井図書館と東京中高年齢労働者福祉センターの建て替え計画。展示・収蔵を担う安定した箱＝Shelter／本やさまざまなアートが並ぶ棚＝Shelf／それらを柔らかく覆うShadeの三層構造をなす。貴重な品を守りながら、街に開かれた多目的でグラデーショナルな建築である。
This project is a reconstruction of the Nerima Art Museum, integrated with the Nukui Library and a labor welfare center. It has a three-layered structure of Shelter, a stable box-like structure for exhibitions and storage; Shelf, lined with books and various artworks; and Shade, forming a soft covering over the other two. While safeguarding valuable items, the building has a multilayered, gradient structure that opens up to the city.

東京都練馬区｜Nerima-ku, Tokyo
美術館、図書館｜museum, library
January 2023－
－
Reinforced concrete ＋ Steel flame
3,270.50m²
8,170.73m²
4 stories, 1 basement

※1 郭旭原聯合建築師事務所と共同設計
※2 株式会社安井建築設計事務所と共同設計
※3 株式会社安井建築設計事務所、株式会社平吹設計事務所、株式会社鈴木建築設計事務所と共同設計
　　協力：アクアバルス建築設計事務所
※4 黄翔龍建築師事務所と共同設計

展覧会出品リスト
List of Works

タイトル・プロジェクト名
種類
材質／技法
サイズ 縦h×幅w／高さh×幅w×奥行きd
（mm）
*展示室Ⅲのガラスケース内作品の表記については、所蔵者の表記に従った。

展示室Ⅰ
からまりしろ―身体の波打ちぎわ

コンセプト写真「蝶々」
写真
アクリル板
700×920

見通せない空間

コンセプト写真「Cabbage」
写真
紙
1,030×1,456

桝屋本店
模型1/50
木、他
200×630×450

ドローイング
トレーシングペーパー、アクリルガッシュ、他
420×297

竣工写真
紙
1,030×727、727×545、545×424

図面
紙
297×210

House H
模型1/50
モルタル、木、他
300×580×490

図面
紙
297×210

Alp
模型1/30
ポリカーボネート、木、他
300×580×490

竣工写真
紙
545×424

図面
紙
210×210

イエノイエ
模型1/100
フェルト、紙、他
60×70×70

竣工写真
紙
424×545

図面
紙
210×210

ひだ

コンセプトスケッチ「Pleats Principle」
紙
1,456×1,030

6/1
実物
布、金属パイプ、他
3,135×6,200×6,850

---

flame frame
実物
アルミ、他
1,450×800×540

Architecture Farm
模型1/50
紙、発泡スチロール、スポンジ、他
400×1,100×590

図面
紙
297×210

模型写真
紙
727×1,030

Gallery S
模型1/50
木、他
450×300×300

模型写真
紙
1,030×727、545×424

図面
紙
297×210

Bloomberg Pavilion
模型1/10
紙、金網、他
800×1,200×1,200

ドローイング
トレーシングペーパー、アクリルガッシュ、
420×297

図面
紙
210×210

竣工写真
紙
1,030×727、394×509

Pleated Sky
模型
スタイロフォーム、アクリル、他
100×550×400

バース
布
4,600×9,200

Csh
モックアップ
発泡スチロール
600×600×600

写真
紙
727×545

ライン

コンセプトスケッチ「Global Bowl concept drawing」
ドローイング
紙、ペン
1,000×1,000

Global Bowl
模型1/2
発泡スチロール、他
1,000×φ2,000

模型1/40
PLA樹脂
75×170×170

モックアップ
集成材
60×1,100×440

竣工写真
紙
727×1,030

図面
紙
297×210

Foam Form
模型1/200
樹脂、他
150×450×300

バース
紙
594×1,210

図面
紙
297×210

LEXUS -amazing flow-
模型1/100
樹脂、他
200×500×350

竣工写真
紙
545×727

図面
紙
297×210

樹

コンセプト写真「tree」
写真
紙
1,456×1,030

Tree-ness House
模型1/50
紙、スチレンボード
600×640×300

ドローイング
紙、色鉛筆、他
210×148

図面
紙
297×210

竣工写真
紙
727×1,030、509×394（3点）

まえばしガレリア
模型1/100
紙、金網、スチレンボード、他
300×800×850

ドローイング
紙、アクリルガッシュ、他
210×148

竣工写真
紙
1,030×727、727×545

図面
紙
297×210

富富話合
模型1/50
木、他
1,700×1,100×510

ドローイング
トレーシングペーパー、アクリルガッシュ、他
420×297

竣工写真
紙
727×1,030

図面
紙
297×210

発酵

発酵コンセプト写真
「Fermanented City」
写真
紙
1,030×1,456

Ryozan Park Green
模型 1/50
紙、発泡スチロール、他
950×300×600

モックアップ
コンクリートキャンバス
1,850×1,800

竣工写真
紙
1,030×727、545×727、424×545、
394×509、509×394

図面
紙
297×210

HARAJUKU Stairs
模型 1/60
木、モルタル、他
400×1,900×1,100

パース
紙
594×1,160

図面
紙
297×210

Taipei Complex
模型 1/50
アクリル、スチレンボード、発泡スチロール、
他
400×900×550

パース
紙
650×1,456

図面
紙
210×210

からまりタイル
実物
粘土、釉薬、他
100×1,820×1,820

9h プロジェクト
各種模型

9h 新大阪
発泡スチロール、紙、プラスチック棒、他
300×30×80

9h 浅草
スチレンボード、紙、他
740×450×210

9h 浜松町
ポリカーボネート、スチレンボード、紙、他
480×105×270

9h 赤坂
ポリカーボネート、スチレンボード、紙、他
500×300×370

9h 半蔵門
ポリカーボネート、スチレンボード、紙、他
425×90×200

9h 名古屋プロポ案
紙、スチレンボード、他
450×110×170

各種竣工写真
紙
1,030×727、394×509（2点）、509×394
（2点）

基隆路プロジェクト
模型
スチレンボード、アクリル、プラスチック棒、
紙、他
900×370×200、（他6点）

華亞案
模型
発泡スチロール、スポンジ、他
180×160×160

Fermented Tower
模型
紙、スチレンボード、スポンジ、他
220×100×160

内湖集合住宅
模型
発泡スチロール、他
130×100×70（他8点）

展示室 II
響き―意識の波打ちぎわ

コンセプトドローイング「響き」
アクリル版
920×920

太田市美術館・図書館
模型 1/50
アクリル、スチレンボード、スノーマット、
ポリカーボネート、発泡スチロール、他
400×1,000×1,000

平田晃久：博士論文『生命論的建築の研究―
〈からまりしろ〉の概念を通して』P.147～
P.164
紙、他
297×210

ワークショップ展示写真
紙、他
500×1,260

ホントカ。小千谷市ひと・まち・文化共創拠点
模型 1/50
スチレンペーパー、紙、他
400×1,000×1,000

ドローイング
紙、他
260×210

動画

フロート模型・アンカー模型・ルーフ模型
紙、木、他
150×3,300×3,200（3点）

練馬区立美術館・貫井図書館
WS1模型（6分割）1/75
スチレンボード、発泡スチロール、木、紙、他
300×1,200×600

WS1模型（2分割）1/75
スチレンボード、発泡スチロール、木、紙、他
400×1,400×1,000

WS2模型（3個）1/300
紙、スチレンボード、他
150×300×200

WS3模型（2個）1/50
発泡スチロール、他
400×2,000×900

敷地模型 1/200
スチレンボード、発泡スチロール、紙、ポリ
カーボネート、他
150×800×1,600

ワークショップ成果品シート（大）
紙、モール、OHPシート、木、他
841×594

ワークショップ成果品シート（小）
紙、モール、OHPシート、木、他
594×420

パース
紙
1,456×1,030、841×1,189、他 計7点

スタディ模型
紙、発泡スチロール、糸、ポリカーボネート、
他
55×245×195、75×300×150、115×
430×230、200×400×400 計52個

太田市風景写真
写真
紙

太田三部作
コンセプト模型（太田市美術館・図書館）
PLA樹脂、アクリル、他
100×200×200

コンセプト模型（Ota lines）
PLA樹脂、アクリル、他
100×200×200

コンセプト模型（太田西複合拠点公共施設建設）
PLA樹脂、アクリル、他
100×300×300

Overlap House
模型 1/50
紙、スチレンボード、他
400×1,800×900

モックアップ
スレート
1,400×3,300

大塚敷地周辺写真
紙

臺灣大學 百歳紀念館
模型 1/100
PLA樹脂、ポリカーボネート、他
300×700×300

ドローイング
トレーシングペーパー、アクリルガッシュ、他
420×297

説明パネル
紙、他
3,200×6,440、3,200×2,800、3,200×
4,560

新竹市中央図書館
模型 1/75
木、アクリル、他
400×5,000×4,000

ドローイング（壁画）
ペンキ、グロスポリマーメディウム、油性ペン
2,850×4,450

BIG-TREE
模型1/100
木、アクリル、スチレンペーパー、針金、他
500×1,200×850

模型1/200
木、発泡スチロール、他
200×600×400

ドローイング
紙、色鉛筆、他
148×210

ドローイング（壁画）
油性ペン
2,950×2,360

Sendai Tree
模型1/100
木、アクリル、ポリカーボネート、スポンジ、他
900×2,000×1,800

コンセプト模型
紙、プラスチック板
80×80×80

パース
紙
550×1,358、550×1,571、550×1,659

展示室 Ⅲ
響きの響き―時空の波打ちぎわ

ガラスケース外

響きの響きコンセプトドローイング
ドローイング
アクリル
920×700

響きの響き
写真：大11枚、小111枚
無機ELシート、半透明紙、他
210×297、104×135

シャイニング・クラウズ
模型1/30
木、他
400×1,000×1,000

ホントカ。
小千谷市ひと・まち・文化共創拠点
模型1/200
モルタル、発泡スチロール、樹脂、他
700×4,000×4,000

EXPO ナショナルデーホール
「レイガーデン」
模型1/135
アクリル、アクリルガッシュ
300×1,400×1,400

守山市伊勢遺跡史跡公園展示施設
模型1/30
PLA樹脂、紙
200×1,400×600

練馬区立美術館・貫井図書館
模型1/75
木、アクリル、他
400×1,200×1,000

HARAKADO
模型1/200
PLA樹脂、ポリカーボネート、発泡スチロール、他
800×5,000×600

臺灣大學 藝文大樓
模型1/100
スチレンペーパー、スチレンボード紙、木、他
600×2,300×1,600

Cloud and Field
模型1/100
アクリル
500×1,200×1,000

八代市民俗伝統芸能伝承館
（お祭りでんでん館）
模型1/50
PLA樹脂、エポキシ樹脂、アクリル、紙、他
200×2,200×1,800

ガラスケース内

重要無形文化財小千谷縮布
「いにしえからの語りかけ」
企画制作者：山岸良三
所蔵：小千谷市
資料協力先：小千谷市にぎわい交流課
1,212×380

越後三山ジオラマ模型
50×300×200

縄文土器　縄文草創期～後期
元中子遺跡（新潟県小千谷市）より出土
所蔵：小千谷市
資料協力先：小千谷市にぎわい交流課
290×290φ

縄文土器　縄文中期
前野遺跡（新潟県小千谷市）より出土
所蔵：小千谷市
資料協力先：小千谷市にぎわい交流課
310×290φ

八ヶ谷戸遺跡出土の大型把手付縄文土器
（区登録有形文化財）
縄文時代中期
所有：練馬区（所蔵：石神井公園ふるさと文化館）
520×230×370

万博コンセプトドローイング
460×600

銅鏡レプリカ
20×250φ

天球儀
300×190φ

原宿の地図
550×320

八代市民俗伝統芸能伝承館 ドローイング
トレーシングペーパー、アクリルガッシュ
297×420

『八代市文化財調査報告書　第9集
妙見祭笠鉾―八代神社祭礼神幸行列笠
鉾等基本調査報告書―』
1996年、八代市教育委員会
書籍
p.234-235
297×210

植物標本（サンショウ・ヤマウコギ）
2024年
340×200、360×220

昆虫標本（ツマベニチョウ・コノハチョウ）
90×80、70×75

鉱物標本
40×140×90、35×50×45、50×80×60、20×90×60、25×100×80

弥生土器
200×120φ

練馬区立美術館・貫井図書館からの富士
ドローイング
トレーシングペーパー、アクリルガッシュ
420×297

富士山ジオラマ模型
80×400×300

復刻版 歌川広重 名所江戸百景
「目黒元富士」
安政4年（2024年復刻制作）
制作：東京伝統木版画工芸協同組合
380×250

復刻版 歌川広重 名所江戸百景
「目黒新富士」
安政4年（2024年復刻制作）
制作：東京伝統木版画工芸協同組合
390×260

伊勢遺跡『祭殿』の「柱根」
棟持柱
弥生時代後期
守山市埋蔵文化財センター
650×240×180、860×220×180

北尾春道「明明庵図面」『茶室の展開図』
1970年、光村推古書院
書籍
p.214-215
370×260

エントランスホール

波打ちぎわの波打ちぎわ
インスタレーション
布、カプセル、音響、他

スケッチブック（12点）
各290×205

太田市美術館・図書館プロポーザル時のスケッチ（2014）
Global Cave 構想時のスケッチ（2015）
Long House 構想時のスケッチ（2012）
Ota Folk Cafe 構想時のスケッチ（2018）
高松市体育館プロポーザル時のスケッチ（2018）
練馬区立美術館・貫井図書館プロポーザル時のスケッチ（2022）
Canon "Prism Liquid" 構想時のスケッチ（2010）
サンティーヴォ・アッラ・サピエンツァ教会のスケッチ（2010）
Kotoriku 構想時のスケッチ（2012）
釜石市復興公営住宅プロポーザル時のスケッチ（2012）
東戸塚教会 建具のスケッチ（2013）
Taipei Roofs 構想時のスケッチ（2013）

HARAKADO
ドローイング
紙、アクリルガッシュ、他
210×148

シャイニング・クラウズ
ドローイング
トレーシングペーパー、アクリルガッシュ、他
420×297

100年後の美術館を想像して

1. 新しい美術館建設を見据えて

1985年10月に開館した練馬区立美術館は、来年の2025年に40周年を迎える。1980年代後半から90年代のおおよそ10年間の「美術館建設ラッシュ」と言われた時期に建設された。区立美術館の先輩は、板橋区立美術館と渋谷区立松濤美術館、そこに練馬が続き、世田谷美術館、目黒区美術館と続く。2016年には墨田区のすみだ北斎美術館も誕生し、特別区という基礎的自治体が保有する美術館が増加している。その他にも、画家などの個人名を冠した区立の記念館が複数館存在する。このことは地方の人々にとってイメージし難いだろうが、区で最も人口の多い世田谷区で約95万人弱、2番手にあたる練馬区で75万人を超える住民を抱えていると言えば、東京の基礎的自治体のポテンシャルが伝わるだろう[1]。それぞれ個性的なコレクションと展覧会を重ね、日本の美術館史、展覧会史にユニークな痕跡を残してきた。

さて当館の場合は、日本近現代美術を中心にという旗印のもと進んできたが、ここ15年ぐらいはそのジャンルも幅を広げ、展覧会の種類も西洋近代美術からポスターなどのグラフィック、浮世絵、いわゆるコンテンポラリーなどと展開している。これは学芸員の専門性や個性と直結している。かなりニッチでマニアックな内容の展覧会を開催したこともしばしばで、その特異性が美術愛好家に受け入れられ、そして美術業界にちょっとした驚きを与えてきたという自負がある。少し偉そうに聞こえるかもしれないが、見る人が見ればわかる面白さという類のものである。

このように独自路線を貫いてきた美術館も、昨今はそれほどのんきなことも言っていられなくなった。たくさんの人々に展覧会を見て欲しいし、近隣の皆様にはぜひとも気軽に立ち寄ってもらいたいと思うが、とりわけ公立美術館は展覧会だけではなく幅広い活動を通して、周辺地域を中心としたあらゆる人々を受け入れる場として門戸を広げるよう求められて久しい。美術作品の保全が美術館の基本的命題であることから、柔軟性を持った様々な活動を能動的に行うことで生じるリスクを考えると、これが簡単なことではないことは想像に難くない。昨今の美術館に求められる空気感は、美術館の姿、在り方を変えてきたと思う。美術作品を愛で、その技巧に驚嘆するだけでなく、新知見を提供する思考の場としての美術館であろうと日々奮闘している学芸員からすれば、「親しみやすい美術館」「まちに役立つ美術館」という看板を背負わされることは、ま

るで美術館の本質と真逆のことを求められているようで、アカデミズムの現場としての折り合いをどうつけるべきか、悩ましいところである。これまで積み重ねてきたような作家や作品研究、受容史、文化史、近代都市の成立など各々の研究成果を生かした展覧会も受動的であると言われてしまえばそれまでで、長年にわたる地道な研究を発表する場を損なうことなく、「私たちの「まち」には美術館がある」と広く認識してもらうためには、ただ発信するだけでなく更に人々の傍に歩み寄るための知恵をしぼる必要があるのだろう。

この難題と向き合う中で建て替えの節目を迎えた練馬区立美術館は、建築家の平田晃久氏にその新しい姿をゆだねることとなった。平田氏は、2017年に開館した群馬県の太田市美術館・図書館で、2022年に日本建築学会賞を受賞している。平田氏のもと、これまでにない美術館と図書館の複合文化施設として生まれ変わることとなる練馬区立美術館は、区内に点在する富士塚から着想を得て、「21世紀の富士塚／アートの雲／本の山」をコンセプトに構想されている。Shelter, Shelf, Shadeの三層構造には、より広い展示室やプロジェクト・ルームなどの小さくとも自由度の高いスペースが設置されて、コレクションを活かした展示も含め、展覧会の可能性を拡大させていくことになる。とりわけ図書館スペースは、本棚の配置によって区切られてできる空間、子どものための小さなスペースや隠れ家的な空間などが様々に入り組んでいて、この建物の顔となっている。そして美術館と図書館をつなげるようなオープン・スペースによって、2つの施設が隔絶されることないように工夫されている。空間的自由度の高い、繋がりを感じる構造には新規性があり、権威的でない姿は新しい美術館像を提示したと言ってもよい。

建物そのものがオープンなイメージの美術館は、「親しみやすい美術館」としての期待感を醸成するだろうし、世間から求められる「これからの美術館像」に悩める学芸員を手助けしてくれるようにも思われる。おおよそ5年後、練馬区立美術館は新しい姿で文化・芸術を発信するベースとして再スタートする。この拠点から美術館が「まち」へと繰り出すこともあれば、人々の集いの場ともなり得るのだろう。学芸員に課せられた宿題は、「まち」との関係性を考えながら、約40年にわたる美術館の歴史を背景に、更なる100年後の美術館のあるべき姿を想像することである。

2. これからのイデオロギー

個人的なことを述べれば、私は2022年10月18日から美術館を離れ、区役所の美術館再整備担当課で新美術館建設の仕事に携わることとなった。主に区民を対象とした5回にわたるワークショップや分科会などの設計事務所との会合を重ねていく中で、新しい美術館が形作られていくのを目の当たりにしてきた。基本設計を通して、一学芸員として思い残したことがないと言えば嘘になる。ただ、紆余曲折を経てどうにか基本設計を終えた今、進行中の実施設計を尻目に、まだ見ぬ新しい美術館に思いをはせながら「平田晃久—人間の波打ちぎわ」展を開催するに至った現在の心境は、想像以上に感慨深い。

「人間の波打ちぎわ」というタイトルに、不可解さを感じた人は少なくないだろう。平田氏は著者の中でも、哲学的思考の中で編み出した造語を駆使して自らの建築について雄弁に語っている。その編み出された造語で、平田建築の核となる言葉が「からまりしろ」である。これを、自然やあらゆる生物の世界が見せる偶発的な「からまり合い」によってのみ形成される形態を消化し、建物に反映する階層構造とでも言うべきか。果たして「人間の波打ちぎわ」と「からまりしろ」は、まったくの別物であるはずもなく、ともに平田建築の世界観を表すこれらを解するために、平田氏の自然や環境を巡る意識にアプローチしたい。

「生命の世界にいきわたる秩序について考えれば考えるほど、それは20世紀に完成を見た近代建築の発想法とは鋭い対立をなすのではないかという思いが強まる。」[2]

平田氏のこの言葉には、胸を突かれたような思いがした。現代の建築家が、人間の科学技術いわゆる文明の発展の証である建築の在り方に自然哲学的、生物学的視点から疑問を投げかけているからだ。そしてこの言葉から、平田氏の建築観について迫るヒントを得たように思った。

平田氏は、近代哲学を代表するドイツの哲学者ゴットフリート・ヴィルヘルム・ライプニッツが、イングランドの数学者で物理学者アイザック・ニュートンの「絶対時間・空間」を批判したことに触れ、時空の哲学から自身の思う建築空間について説いている。ライプニッツの「関係説」への言及は、平田氏の空間に対する根本的な思想を表明しているように思われる。そもそも「関係説」は、「観念的な時空は、事物の関係から構成される」とする考え方である。

つまり、実体があるわけではなく、時間と空間は、事物の関係—これを因果関係とでも言うべきか—からのみ構成されるとする。平田氏は、このライプニッツの空間に対する考え方を、建築に当てはめることができると言う。どのフロアも同様に設計された均質なビルは、その階層は原理上では無限に増やすことができ、これはニュートンの絶対空間的な無限に広がる均質な空間の理念である。しかし実際には、建築物は単体で成立するものではなく、取り巻く外部環境との関係性、つまり、事物の因果関係において成立している。故に、その建物が周囲にどのように影響しているかという「関係性＝環境」[3]を考えていく必要がある。それは地球という有限の空間の中に、人も建築物も存在するからだ。ともに存在する以上は、有限の空間で「環境」への作用がより良いものでなくてはならない。

このライプニッツの関係説に導かれた平田氏の思考で、最も興味深いのは建築物を巡る空間への言説が「環境問題」に繋がっていくことである。階層構造を指す「からまりしろ」の概念からもわかるように、平田氏は人間の営みを他の生命のそれと切り離して考えない。つまり「環境」について考えることは、「生命の世界にいきわたる秩序」について考えることである。それは、「からまりしろ」を発見するに至った平田氏の根源的な自然観、生命観、あるいは世界観にアプローチすることである。「近代以降の際限ない成長のようなものが、明らかな限界に達している。」[4]という平田氏の問題意識は、「成長」という強迫観念に追い立てられている我々の常識そのものを覆す必要があると提唱しているように聞こえる。「成長」への疑問が「環境問題」を考えることに直結することは容易に想像が付くが、平田氏は「環境」について具体的な事象を挙げて意識するだけでなく、「思考の枠組みの問題」[5]として根本的に捉え直すことが必要であると主張する。それは、そもそも自然、動物、人間などの関係性をどのように捉えるかということ、まずは「生命の世界にいきわたる秩序」をどのように認識するか、ということであろうと解釈すれば、現代人の思考を築いた根源を訪ねてみれば答えが得られるに違いない。

西洋化された現代社会に生きる私たちの自然認識が構築されたプロセスを知るには、近代合理主義哲学において「人間」と「自然」の関係性がどのように考えられたか、教科書的おさらいが有効である。まず「近代哲学の祖」とされるフランスの哲学者ルネ・デカルトは、「心身二元論」を通して人間の本質は精神にあり、身

体は機械的なものとみなした。肉体は精神の器に過ぎず、「精神と身体は別の存在である」と唱えたのである。そして、この肉体が機械に過ぎないという点においてのみ人間と動物の間に類似性は認められるが、「神」の似姿である人間は、精神を持つため他のあらゆる生物よりも優位であるとする。人間は唯一、「神」との特別な繋がりの証である精神を持っているが、それ以外の生物、つまり動物や植物は、物質にすぎず精神も意思も持たず、思考もできないと言う。このキリスト教的世界観と合致した人間中心主義的理屈に則ると、人間以外の生物は単なる物質となり、支配される対象となった。この観念はその後の主流を占め、自然観、科学観に圧倒的な影響を与えている。

さて、このデカルトの「心身二元論」、機械論的自然観に対したのが、オランダの哲学者バールーフ・デ・スピノザである。スピノザは、精神も身体も「神」のうちにあるとする同一実体における2つの本質、つまり精神と身体はひとつだと主張し、「心身平行論」を説いた。「人間は精神と身体とから成り、そして人間身体は我々がそれを感ずるとおりに存在する、ということになる。」[6] つまり、「神」、人間、その精神や魂、自然、動物、それぞれは異なる存在として認識されているかもしれないが、すべての事物に内在的原因としての「神」が宿っている。あらゆる事物の様態が「神」の変容であり、「神すなわち自然」という汎神論的理論を展開した。人間は自然、他の生物と同等であり、我々の魂も精神も物質と同じであるということは、創造物のすべての観念を「神」が有しているのだ。

デカルト的概念は様々に補強されて、動物も自然も人間の身体すらも物質として捉えることで、すべてを資源や労働力として見なすことを肯定した。それは未知の土地へ侵入し、自然を切り開き、人を機械のように働かせることへの躊躇を失くした。経済や産業の「成長」には、極めて有用に働いたのである。資本主義が誕生した近代以降、私たちはあらゆる分野において「成長」を信じて進んできたし、その只中に置かれて久しいにも関わらず、なお「成長」を目途にしている。この「成長主義」によって生じている問題は数知れず指摘されているが、有限の資源が制限なく消費されることから、最も深刻な問題は環境破壊であるだろう。ここで先述の、永遠と続くように見える「成長」への不安を投げかけた平田氏の言葉を思い出してもらいたい。ライプニッツを通して、有限の空間という認識、外部環境と建物との関係性、それが「環境問題」へと繋がっていた。そして、自然や生物が織りなす光景に着想する「からまりしろ」の

概念、人間とあらゆる動物そして自然との間に主従をつくらない発想からはスピノザ的自然観を思い起こさせる。ただ、これはあくまでも西洋的思想に則った場合の話であって、私たち日本人からすればスピノザのように人間と自然を同等の存在とする考え方には、本来なじみがあることに触れておきたい。

元来、神国であった日本に仏教が伝来し、神仏融合という日本独自の思想が育ったことにより、古代から続く自然崇拝が日本文化の根源として定着した。それは草花や動物などあらゆる生物に神性が宿り、仏性があると信じられるようになったということである。つまりは、木を切ることは命を取ることで罰当たりであったし、鳥の声が仏法を説いているとも理解された。人間が自然を支配するのではなく、あらゆる生物が同等の生命として共存するという考え方は、日本人にとって慣れ親しんだもので、西洋近代思想の移入後においても失われてはいない。現代でも、とりわけ自然から生活の糧を得ている人々は海や山に神を見出して祀っているし、飼っていた昆虫が亡くなれば墓を作ってその命を供養した幼い頃の思い出を誰しもが持っているだろう。アニミズムと仏教的教義から、支配関係にない人間と自然、生物との関係性が根源的に築かれている日本人にとっては、スピノザの汎神論的自然観を抵抗なく理解できるのではないか。もちろん同様の自然観は、日本独自の物ではなく、アジアの各地、アメリカン・インディアンの文化などにも見られる。近代化の中で日本人が西洋的思想を学び、身に着けてきたとはいえ、異なる文化的背景を持つ西洋人と同様の感性で物事を捉えることはできない。平田氏の建築を巡る思想は、日本の文化的背景に裏打ちされた無意識的な自然観にも導かれているように思われる。

資源や資本、労働力の上に成り立つ建築家が「環境問題」を意識し、「成長主義」を疑うことは、今という時代に不可欠な視点であると同時に、大いなる矛盾もはらんでいる。しかし、現代の日本において最も注目される建築家のひとりである平田晃久氏の主張する建築思想が、私たちのイデオロギーに揺さぶりをかける先進的なものであることは間違いない。「成長」には限界があり、資源も地球も空間も有限であると人々に再認識を促し、未来の建築のあるべき姿を示すことは、平田氏自身が負っている課題である。そして私たちはこの建築家に希望を託すだけではなく、立ち止まり、ひたすらに進むことだけが本質的な幸福ではないと、有限のものを大切にしながら、これからのイデオロギーを作り上げていかねばならない。

小野寛子（練馬区立美術館　学芸員）

註

1. 「東京都の人口（推計）」の概要（令和6年6月1日現在）を参照。
https://www.metro.tokyo.lg.jp/tosei/hodohappyo/press/2024/06/26/18.html
2. 平田晃久『現代建築家コンセプト・シリーズ8　平田晃久　建築とは〈からまりしろ〉をつくることである』LIXIL出版、2011年、20頁。
3. 同書、24頁。
4. 同書、6頁。
5. 同書、26頁。
6. スピノザ、畠中尚志訳『エチカ（上）』岩波文庫、1951年、109頁。

Nerima Art Museum and Nukui Library

Envisioning the Museum a Century from Now

1. Expectations for the New Museum

The Nerima Art Museum opened its doors in October 1985, and marks its 40th anniversary next year. Built during Japan's approximately 10-year "museum construction boom" of the late 1980s and early 1990s, it is one of a series of museums operated by wards of Tokyo, built after the Itabashi Art Museum and Shoto Museum of Art and before the Setagaya Art Museum and Meguro Museum of Art, Tokyo. In 2016, the opening of the Sumida Hokusai Museum further expanded the roster of ward-operated museums, and there are several other museums run by wards that are dedicated to individual artists. While it may be difficult for those outside the metropolitan area to envision, the populations of many of Tokyo's wards easily equal those of independent cities, with Nerima, at more than 750,000 residents, second only to Setagaya with nearly 950,000.[1] With numbers like these, there is clearly further potential for museums operated by the municipalities (wards) that make up Tokyo. Each museum has continued to pursue distinctive collections and exhibitions, and has made unique contributions to the history of museums and exhibitions in Japan.

The Nerima Art Museum has primarily focused on modern and contemporary Japanese art, but over the past 15 years, it has broadened its scope to include a diverse array of exhibitions, from Western modern art to posters and other graphics, ukiyo-e, and cutting-edge contemporary art. This expansion reflects the expertise and originality of the curatorial team. It frequently holds exhibitions featuring niche and esoteric content, which has resonated well with art enthusiasts and at times surprised the art world. While it might sound a bit pretentious to say so, the museum prides itself on presenting things that appeal to the discerning viewer.

While it has consistently charted its own course, the museum can no longer afford to adopt the somewhat complacent stance I have just described. It aims both to attract large audiences to exhibitions and to encourage local residents to drop by casually. For quite a while now, public-sector museums in particular have faced increasing demands to go beyond merely holding exhibitions, and to open their doors wider and engage with a diverse range of people, especially in the local community, through various activities. In light of a museum's fundamental mandate to preserve works of art, the risks associated with flexibly and actively undertaking a wide variety of activities are clearly considerable. People's evolving expectations of museums have altered their operations and their nature. Curators are challenged daily to make museums serve as inspirational spaces that deliver new insights, not merely venues to admire art or marvel at the skills of artists. The roles of "a broadly accessible museum" and "a museum that reaches out to the community" can be burdensome, as they can seem thoroughly at odds with a museum's essential duty, and fulfilling these roles in tandem with traditional, more academic functions is a complex balancing act. Thus far, museums have presented exhibitions grounded in research on artists and their works, the history of their reception, cultural history, the development of the modern city and so forth, but if the presentation of these exhibitions is deemed too passive, then the challenge is to make them engaging without compromising years of meticulous research. To truly embed the museum as a vital part of our community, it is essential not only to share information, but also to find innovative ways of connecting more closely with the public.

Amid these challenges, the Nerima Art Museum is approaching a major milestone with its reconstruction, and the new design has been entrusted to architect Akihisa Hirata. He is the recipient of the Architectural Institute of Japan Award in 2022 for the Art Museum & Library, Ota, opened in 2017 in Gunma Prefecture. Hirata will transform the museum into a new kind of composite cultural facility that integrates an art museum and a library. , designed with the concepts of "a 21st century Fujitsuka / Clouds of Art / Mountains of Books," drawing inspiration from Fujitsuka (mini-Mount Fuji mounds) scattered across the ward. Its three-tiered structure, termed "Shelter, Shelf, Shade," will broaden possibilities for exhibitions, including more effective use of the collection, through a combination of larger galleries and a smaller, adapted space called "Project Room." The library area will notably feature a variety of intricately arranged spaces defined by bookshelf placement, including cozy areas and hidden nooks for children, which will be a defining element of the building. The design ingeniously links the museum and the library through open spaces, ensuring seamless integration of the two facilities. The structure's spatial flexibility and interconnectedness offer fresh perspectives, projecting a non-authoritative image that could redefine our future vision for museums.

The building's open design will enhance the perception of the Nerima Art Museum as "a broadly accessible museum," and will surely aid curators grappling with public expectations for the role of museums moving forward. About five years from now, the new Nerima Art Museum will relaunch as a hub for dissemination of local culture and art. As a base that extends its activities outward into the surrounding area, the museum has the potential to become a new gathering place for the community. The task for curators is to envision the museum's future a hundred years from now, in light of its relationship with the community and its nearly 40-year history thus far.

2. Ideologies for a Sustainable Future

Personally, on October 18, 2022 I moved from the museum to the ward office's Art Museum Redevelopment Division, where I am involved in the new museum's construction on the administrative side. Through a series of five workshops and subcommittee meetings primarily aimed at Nerima residents, I have witnessed the shaping of the new facility. It would be dishonest to claim that I have had no regrets or misgivings throughout the basic design process. However, with the basic design now completed after many twists and turns, and with the detailed design process ongoing, my mental state as we prepare for *Architecture Arises at the Water's Edge for Human Beings* is more emotional, with regard to the as-yet-unseen new museum, than I could have imagined.

The title *Architecture Arises at the Water's Edge for Human Beings* might initially puzzle many. In his writings, Hirata discusses his architecture eloquently, coining neologisms and placing his approach in philosophical context. A term central to Hirata's architecture is "tangling base," which describes hierarchical structures that replicate forms created by accidental entanglements found in nature and among all living things. These forms are reflected in his architectural designs. Indeed, the "water's edge" and "tangling base" are not unrelated, and both articulate Hirata's architectural worldview. For this reason, in the remainder of this essay I would like to discuss Hirata's perceptions of nature and the environment.

"The more I ponder the order pervading the living world, the more starkly it seems to contrast with the ideology of modern architecture that became firmly entrenched in the 20th century."[2]

These words from Hirata keenly struck a chord with me. They represent a contemporary architect challenging the conventional view of architecture as emblematic of the scientific and technological progress of human civilization, through a lens of natural philosophy and biology. And these words offer a sharp focus on Hirata's architectural discourse.

Hirata discusses the German philosopher Gottfried Wilhelm Leibniz's critique of the English mathematician and physicist Isaac Newton's concept of "absolute time and space," and how this philosophical debate over space-time shapes his own approach to architectural spaces. His reference to Leibniz's "relational theory" seems to point to core of Hirata's philosophy of architecture. This theory states that space and time are not physical properties but are defined by relationships, which might be described as causal, among objects. Hirata draws on this theory to inform his understanding of architectural space, positing that architecture should not be seen in isolation but as part of a broader context. For instance, a building with uniformly designed floors might theoretically expand upward indefinitely. It is the notion of an infinitely expanding uniform space as in Newtonian absolute space. However, in reality, a building does not exist in isolation; its design and function is intimately tied to its surroundings, that is to the causal relationships between objects. Thus, Hirata emphasizes the importance of "relationality = environment,"[3] i.e. of considering a building's impact on its surroundings. On a planet where both people and buildings occupy finite space, their coexistence is crucial and ought to affect the environment positively.

Most intriguingly, Hirata's ideas, guided by Leibniz's relational theory, link spatial discourse around architecture directly to environmental issues. His concept of a hierarchical structure as a "tangling base" illustrates his view that human activities cannot be isolated from those of other living things. In other words, considering environmental means considering "the order pervading the living world." This approach defines Hirata's fundamental views of nature, life, and the world, which led to his development of the "tangling base" concept. Hirata's critical observation that "the unbounded growth of the modern era has clearly reached its limits"[4] challenges the prevailing obsession with perpetual growth. It is easy to make a direct connection between questioning growth and cosidering the environment issues, but Hirata argues that addressing environmental issues goes beyond citing specific things, events, and phenomena as problematic, and involves fundamentally reshaping "systemic frameworks of thought."[5] This necessitates a profound reevaluation of how we understand relationships among nature, animals, and humans, and fundamentally, how we perceive "the order pervading the living world." Revisiting the foundational beliefs that have molded modern thought is sure to lead us to deeper understanding.

To grasp how perceptions of nature have been constructed in Westernized modern societies, we can benefit from a textbook-style review of key ideas in modern rationalist philosophy regarding the relationship between humanity and nature. René Descartes, the French philosopher often called the father of modern philosophy, posited "mind-body dualism," asserting that the essence of a human being resides in the mind and relegating the body to a mere mechanical function. This view framed the body as merely a vessel for the mind, the two being separate entities. Within this framework, similarities

between human and animal were acknowledged only in terms of "mechanical" bodily functions. Humans, portrayed as being made in God's image and endowed with a mind, were considered superior to all other life forms. The human mind was cited as evidence that we alone have a spiritual connection to God, while other living things, i.e. animals and plants, were reduced to mere material lacking spirit, will, or capacity for thought. This anthropocentric mindset, which aligns with the Christian worldview, relegated all non-human entities to the status of matter to be dominated. This perspective subsequently permeated mainstream thought, exerting an overwhelming influence on how nature and science are perceived.

The Dutch philosopher Baruch Spinoza countered Descartes's "mind-body dualism" and mechanistic view of nature, advocating for the unity of mind and body as two inseparable manifestations of a single entity within the kingdom of God. This idea forms the basis of his "mind-body parallelism" doctrine. Spinoza's declaration that "man consists of mind and body, and that the human body exists according as we feel it"[6] encapsulates his belief that entities we perceive as distinct – God, man, the mind, the soul, nature, animals – are in fact all inhabited by God as an immanent cause. He developed a pantheistic worldview asserting that everything is intrinsically God, the immanent cause of all things, in different forms, as expressed by the Latin phrase *Deus, sive Natura* (God, or Nature.) According to Spinoza, humans are on equal footing with nature and other living beings. He argued that our souls and minds are not distinct from matter, and that all ideas in existence are manifestations of God.

Descartes's dogma has been reinforced in all kinds of ways, framing animals, nature, and even the human body as mere matter, and affirming the view of all things as exploitable as resources or labor. This removed any potential reservations about invading uncharted territories, devastating the natural environment, and mechanizing human labor. This has, of course, been highly beneficial for the growth of economies and industry. Since the advent of capitalism, we have embraced growth as the highest good in all fields, and while this mindset has been entrenched for centuries now, we are still hungrily pursuing yet more growth. Problems arising from this growth-centric ideology are innumerable and well-documented, with environmental destruction due to unrestricted consumption of finite resources being the most urgent. Here let us recall Hirata's words, quoted earlier, voicing concerns about unending growth. His recognition of space as finite, and perception of relationships between buildings and external environments, informed by Leibniz, connects to environmental issues. Meanwhile, his "tangling base" paradigm, inspired by the complex interplay of nature and living organisms, and the rejection of hierarchical distinctions between humanity, other animals, and the natural world, reverberate with Spinoza's view of nature. It should be noted, however, that this discourse is rooted in Western thought. For us in Japan, the notion of viewing humans and nature as equals, as Spinoza advocated, ought to be intrinsically familiar.

When Buddhism was introduced to Japan, a land that its inhabitants believed to be divine, it fostered a unique syncretism between Buddhism and the indigenous faith of Shinto, entrenching the nature worship that was a foundational element of Japanese culture. This led to the belief that all living beings, including plants and animals, possess divinity and Buddha nature. Consequently, cutting a tree was deemed the sinful taking of a life, while the singing of birds was interpreted as preaching of Buddhist doctrine. Rather than dominating nature, the Japanese embraced the concept of coexisting as equals with all life, a notion that has endured despite the influx of the Western thought that has dominated the modern era. Even today, many who depend on nature for their livelihood continue to revere deities in seas and mountains, and many Japanese have childhood memories of making graves for pet insects to honor their lives. Given this deep-rooted relationship with nature, shaped by animism and Buddhist teachings and devoid of hierarchical distinctions, Spinoza's pantheistic worldview is intuitively understandable to the Japanese. This perspective is of course not unique to Japan, but is also prevalent in various Asian regions, Native American cultures and elsewhere. Despite embracing

modernization and Western ideologies, the Japanese, due to their distinct cultural backgrounds, perceive the world differently from Westerners. Hirata's architectural thinking appears influenced by this subconscious, culturally ingrained view of nature.

Architecture is built upon resources, capital, and labor, and in the present era, it is both vital and paradoxical for architects to confront environmental issues and question the ideology of unending growth. However, Akihisa Hirata, one of the most prominent architects in Japan today, unmistakably challenges prevailing ideologies with his innovative approach. As an advocate for recognizing the limits to growth and the finite nature of resources, our planet, and space, Hirata shoulders the responsibility of pointing the way to the future of architecture. As for the rest of us, we must do more than simply place our hopes in architects such as Hirata. Recognizing that relentless progress is not synonymous with genuine happiness, we must cherish the finite, while forging new ideologies for a sustainable future.

Hiroko Ono
Curator, Nerima Art Museum

Notes:
1. Ref. "Overview of the Population of Tokyo (Estimated) (as of June 1, 2024)":
   https://www.metro.tokyo.lg.jp/tosei/hodohappyo/press/2024/06/26/18.html
2. Akihisa Hirata, *Contemporary Architects Concept Series 8: Akihisa Hirata – Architecture is Creating a "Tangling Base,"* LIXIL Publishing, 2011, p. 20.
3. Ibid., p. 24.
4. Ibid., p. 6.
5. Ibid., p. 26.
6. Spinoza, *Ethics*, J.M. Dent & Sons Ltd, 1910, p. 92

練馬の富士塚をめぐる

富士山登拝と同じ御利益のある小さなお山

それぞれの地域で「お富士さん」という名で親しまれることとなる小さなお山・富士塚が、江戸時代後期以降、江戸東京のあちこちに誕生する。富士山の黒ボク石（溶岩）で表面が覆われ、ジグザグに曲がりくねった登山道や合目石、小御嶽神社、烏帽子岩、浅間神社、御胎内といった、富士山を構成する要素や信仰にまつわる場所が、ものの見事に表現されている。単なる富士山の“ような”山ではない、富士山の“写し”、それが富士塚である。

　古代より富士山は、荒ぶる山、聖なる山として扱われてきたが、江戸時代に庶民の中で富士信仰が広がり、今日に通じるような身近な存在へと変わっていった。この富士信仰の礎を築いたのが、富士講の開祖とされる戦国時代末期の行者・長谷川角行で、角行の流れを受け継ぎ、普及のきっかけをつくったのが、徳川吉宗の時代に活躍した食行身禄である。彼は富士信仰の教えを分かりやすく庶民に説き、当時の政治への抗議として、享保18（1733）年、富士山の七合五勺の烏帽子岩で断食の末に入定する。この出来事をきっかけに富士信仰が爆発的に広まり、「江戸八百八講」といわれるほど、いくつもの富士講が誕生する。

　富士講とは、費用を持ち寄り、順番に数名が交代で代表して富士山を登拝することを目的とした富士山を信仰する人々の集まりである。そして、入山禁止であった女性や子どもをはじめ、誰でも富士山に登る体験ができるようにと富士講によって生み出されたのが、富士塚なのである。

　安永8（1779）年、身禄の弟子で植木職人であった高田藤四郎による高田水稲荷神社境内につくられた高田富士から富士塚の歴史は始まる。身禄ゆかりの吉田口からの景観を模した造形で、頂上からは富士山を眺め拝むことができる。疑似的な富士山登拝により、実際の富士山登拝と同じ御利益を得ることができるとされ、瞬く間に庶民の心を掴む存在となっていった。その後、江戸後期から昭和初期にかけて多くの富士塚が築造され、都内には現在でも60を超える富士塚がある。

　それでは、東京都練馬区内にある4つの富士塚を巡りながら、その姿についてもう少し詳しく見てみよう。

江古田の富士塚

商店街や学生の街として有名な西武池袋線江古田駅、その駅前にある浅間神社に「江古田の富士塚」はある。高さ約8m、径約30mと比較的規模も大きく、下練馬村・中新井村・中村の各講から成る小竹丸祓講による天保10（1839）年または文化年間（1804-1818）の築造とされ、大正12（1923）年の関東大震災によって損壊したが、翌年復旧工事が行われている。

　登山道入口には向かい合って合掌する二匹の猿がいる。合目石が置かれたジグザグの登山道には講紋が刻まれた石碑や石灯籠が数多く配され、山の表面は黒ボクで覆われている。中腹には経ヶ岳の石碑や烏天狗と大天狗、小御嶽神社碑があり、山頂には唐破風屋根を持つ石宮が設置されている。山全体が鬱蒼とした樹木で囲まれていて、今日の富士塚の山頂に立つと、全方位緑に包まれる中、江古田の街の喧騒から解き放たれた、静寂かつ神秘的な空気を感じることができる。築造時とは社会も環境も変化する中、都市空間の中の緑に囲まれた富士山として存在するその異質さも、都市の中の富士塚としての魅力のひとつではないだろうか。

下練馬の富士塚

東武東上線東武練馬駅を出て南へ、ここは旧川越街道の下練馬宿だった地域で、今も宿場町特有の短冊状の敷地割が残っている。そんな歴史を持つ商店街の中に「下練馬の富士塚」は突如として現れる。高さ約5m、径約15mの大きさで、下練馬村上宿・中宿の丸吉講によるもの。築造年代は不明であるが、明治5（1872）年に再築、関東大震災で崩壊後、昭和2（1927）年に再々築されている。

　こちらの猿像、片方は御幣を持ち、もう片方は合掌し、何とも愛くるしい表情をしている。ジグザグの登山道を進むと、中腹あたりに小御嶽神社がある。その手前では、剣を持った烏天狗と羽扇を持った大天狗が向かい合っている。山頂には石宮のほか、富士山の方角を示した印と「標高37.76m」と刻まれた標識がある。この山の標高はちょうど富士山の1/100となっていて、猿や天狗の丸みを帯びたその姿も含めて心をくすぐる要素が多い。街道沿いの宿場町の富士塚として、その立地も興味深い。

氷川神社富士塚

東武東上線下赤塚駅から歩いて約10分、今度は住宅地の中、氷川神社の境内階段脇にひっそりとあるのは「氷川神社富士塚」である。これまでのようないわゆる山を築いたものではなく、斜面を巧みに利用して山としたタイプである。元からある地形をうまく活かした富士塚は都内にもいくつか存在し、山の築き方もそれぞれに違いを見つけることができる。

　高さ約4m、径約15mの大きさを持ち、丸吉講によるもので、築造年代は明らかではないが、天保年間（1830-1844）の築造の可能性もある。麓から見るとそれなりの大きさを感じるが、裏側から見ると、石宮がちょこんとのった程度の盛土にしか感じられず、必ずしも360度、山としての姿があるわけではないことがまた、富士塚の面白いところでもある。

中里の富士塚

最後は、練馬区大泉町にある「中里の富士塚」である。これまでの3つの富士塚と異なり、稲荷山憩いの森やカタクリ群生地である清水山の森など、白子川沿いの自然豊かな環境の中にある。八坂神社の社殿に向かって右手、こちらも斜面をうまく利用して築かれているため、正面となる南側の麓から見上げた大きさは格別である。南側基部からは高さ約12m、径約30mで、丸吉講による明治初期の築造とされているが、文政5（1822）年の石碑があり、江戸時代にはその原型があったと思われる。

　ジグザグの登山道の各所に配されている石造物の種類も豊富で、鈴原神社、道祖神碑、経ヶ嶽、亀磐、宝永山、小御岳（嶽）神社、烏帽子岩、駒ヶ嶽、剣ヶ峰（けんがみね）などのほか、裾野には胎内横穴もある。山頂からは家々が連なる景色を眺めることができるが、あたり一面田畑だった頃を想像すると、その景色は圧巻で、今よりも山としての存在感が強くあったのではないだろうか。どっしりとしたその佇まいは、都市とは異なる農村の中の富士塚ならではの姿ともいえる。

一口に富士塚と言っても、同じ姿かたちをしたものはなく、その構成要素や歴史、周辺の環境などは、実に様々である。富士塚そのものの姿を観察することはもちろん、富士塚周辺へと視野を広げることで、さらに富士塚の持つ歴史的、文化的な価値や個性が見えてくる。

　　　　　　　　根岸博之（公益財団法人 練馬区文化振興協会）

江古田の富士塚｜東京都練馬区小竹町1-59-2 浅間神社境内（左上）、下練馬の富士塚｜東京都練馬区北町2-41 浅間神社境内（右上）、氷川神社富士塚｜東京都練馬区北町8-22 氷川神社境内（左下）、中里の富士塚｜東京都練馬区大泉町1-44 八坂神社脇（右下）

参考文献
・『練馬の富士塚　民俗文化財の記録2』練馬区教育委員会、1984年
・『練馬の神社　三訂版　郷土史シリーズNo.5』練馬区教育委員会、2000年
・『富士山　江戸・東京と練馬の富士』練馬区立石神井公園ふるさと文化館、2015年

The Fujizuka of Nerima

Miniature Mountains that Bring the Blessings of a Mount Fuji Pilgrimage

After the late Edo period (1603-1868), small hills known as Fujizuka ("Fuji mounds"), affectionately referred to as O-Fuji-san by locals, were constructed throughout Edo (now Tokyo). These hills were covered in *kuroboku-ishi* (volcanic rock from Mount Fuji) and reproduced numerous features of the mountain: zigzagging paths, *gome-ishi* (stones marking the 10 stations of Mount Fuji), Komitake Shrine, Eboshi-iwa Rock (named for its resemblance to a type of hat), Sengen Shrine, and O*tainai* (sacred womb-like tunnels). These mirrored not only the physical characteristics of Mount Fuji but also its spiritual significance, making them not mere approximations or replicas, but embodiments of Fuji itself.

Since ancient times, Mount Fuji has been regarded as both a tempestuous and sacred mountain. During the Edo period, Fuji-shinko (the worship of Mount Fuji, involving climbing the mountain as a religious pilgrimage) became popular among the common people, and it became the iconic presence that it remains to this day. The roots of this folk belief can be traced back to Hasegawa Kakugyo, a religious ascetic in the late Sengoku period (roughly the late 15th and 16th centuries), who is considered the founder of Fuji-ko. Following in Kakugyo's footsteps, Jikigyo Miroku, active during the reign of Tokugawa Yoshimune, paved the way for Fuji-shinko's popularization among the public. In a protest against the political climate of his time, he fasted at Eboshi-iwa Rock between the seventh and eighth stations of Mount Fuji in 1733, leading to his death. This fueled the rapid expansion of Fuji-shinko, leading to the formation of what were known as 808 Fuji-ko (magico-religious societies centered on Mount Fuji) in Edo. In the Japanese tradition, "808" is used as a stand-in for "a very large number."

Fuji-ko were groups of people who pooled resources and took turns climbing Mount Fuji as representatives of the entire group. Fujizuka were constructed by Fuji-ko to allow women and children, traditionally barred from climbing Mount Fuji, and others unable to climb it, to have a simulated experience of ascending Fuji.

The history of Fujizuka goes back to 1779, when Takada Fuji was constructed on the grounds of Takada Mizu-inari Shrine by Takada Toshiro, a gardener and disciple of Jikigyo Miroku. Modeled on the view from the Yoshida-guchi route associated with Miroku, the mini-mountain's design enabled visitors to view and worship the actual Mount Fuji from its summit. Believed to bestow the same spiritual blessings as an actual pilgrimage up Mount Fuji, these simulated climbs rapidly won the hearts of the populace. Numerous Fujizuka continued to be constructed until the early Showa era (1926-1989), with over 60 still existing in Tokyo today.

Now, let's take a closer look at the four Fujizuka located in Nerima, Tokyo.

Ekoda Fujizuka

Ekoda Fujizuka is located on the grounds of Sengen Shrine next to Ekoda Station on the Seibu Ikebukuro line, in an area known for its bustling shopping streets and vibrant student population. This Fujizuka is relatively large, about eight meters in height with a diameter of roughly 30 meters. It was constructed either in 1839 or during the Bunka era (1804-1818) by the Kotakemaru-harai Fuji-ko federation, consisting of Fuji-ko societies from Shimo-Nerima Village, Naka'arai-mura Village, and Nakamura Village. It was damaged by the Great Kanto Earthquake in 1923, but underwent restoration the following year.

At the entrance to the climbing path, two monkeys face each other in a gesture of prayer. The zigzagging path is lined with station-marking stones, many stone monuments bearing the Fuji-ko crest, and numerous stone lanterns. The surface of the mountain is covered in *kuroboku-ishi* (volcanic rock from Mount Fuji). Midway up, there is a stone monument representing Mount Kyogatake and figures of greater (long-nosed) and lesser (raven) *tengu* (mountain-dwelling demigods), along with a Komitake Shrine stone. At the summit stands a stone shrine with a *karahafu* curved-gable roof. The Fujizuka is encircled by a dense grove of trees, and the summit today is a quiet sanctuary enveloped in greenery, with a serene and mystical atmosphere detached from the urban bustle of Ekoda. The uniqueness of this urban Fujizuka, nestled within urban greenery, adds to its allure, as it continues to symbolize Mount Fuji amid a society and environment that has radically changed since it was built.

Shimo-Nerima Fujizuka

Exiting Tobu-Nerima Station on the Tobu Tojo Line and heading south, one enters what was once the Shimo-Nerima post-town on the old Kawagoe Route, where narrow, strip-like plots of land typical of post-towns still remain. Along the area's historic shopping street, Shimo-Nerima Fujizuka suddenly emerges. This Fujizuka stands approximately five meters tall, with a diameter of about 15 meters, and was constructed by the Marukichi Fuji-ko society from Kamijuku and Nakajuku of Shimo-Nerima Village. The original construction date is unknown, but it was rebuilt in 1872, collapsed during the Great Kanto Earthquake, and was reconstructed again in 1927.

At this site, one monkey statue holds a staff adorned with plaited paper streamers, while the other clasps its hands in prayer, both with endearing facial expressions. Ascending the zigzagging path, one encounters Komitake Shrine halfway up the hill. Near it, a lesser (raven) *tengu* wielding a sword faces a greater (long-nosed) *tengu* holding a feathered fan. At the summit, in addition to a stone shrine, there is a marker pointing towards Mount Fuji and another engraved with "Elevation 37.76m," which is exactly 1/100th of Mount Fuji's elevation (summit's height above sea level). The whimsical figures of the monkeys and *tengu*, along with the signage, lend a playful element to this Fujizuka, and its location in a former post-town along an ancient route is intriguing.

Hikawa Shrine Fujizuka

About a 10-minute walk from Shimo-Akatsuka Station on the Tobu Tojo Line is Hikawa Shrine Fujizuka, nestled quietly in a residential area beside the staircase of the Hikawa Shrine precincts. Unlike typical Fujizuka, which are mounds constructed from scratch, this one capitalizes on the natural terrain, cleverly utilizing an existing slope to form a hill. Several other Fujizuka in Tokyo ingeniously employ geographical features, with each featuring unique construction methods.

The work of the Marukichi Fuji-ko society, this Fujizuka is approximately four meters in height, with a diameter of about 15 meters. While the exact date of its construction remains unclear, it may have been built between 1830 and 1844. From the front it appears to be of imposing size, but from the back it seems merely like a mound of earth topped with a stone shrine, and it does not fully maintain the appearance of a mini-mountain from all 360 degrees. This adds an interesting dimension to this Fujizuka.

Nakazato Fujizuka

The final Fujizuka on our tour is Nakazato Fujizuka, located in Oizumi-machi. Unlike the previous three, it stands in lush natural surroundings along the Shiroko-gawa River, close to woods like Inariyama Ikoi-no-mori and Shimizuyama-no-mori, the latter famous for its clusters of Japanese fawn lilies. Located to the right of Yasaka Shrine's main hall, this Fujizuka takes advantage of the natural sloping terrain, enhancing its grandeur when viewed from the front, i.e. the southern base. It stands about 12 meters tall, with a diameter of about 30 meters. It was constructed in the early Meiji era (1868-1912) by the Marukichi Fuji-ko society, but a stone monument dated 1822 indicates that a prototype may have existed in the Edo period (1603-1868).

This Fujizuka features a diverse array of stone structures along its zigzagging paths, including Suzuhara Shrine, Dosojin stone markers, Mount Kyogatake, Kameiwa Rock, Mount Hoei, Komitake Shrine, Eboshi-iwa Rock, Mount Komagatake, Kengamine Peak, and a *tainai* (sacred womb-like tunnel) at its base. From the summit there is a view of rows of houses, but imagining the area as it once was, covered with fields and farms, gives a sense of the formidable presence the mountain must have had. The imposing appearance of Nakazato Fujizuka makes it stand out as a rural Fujizuka, differing in character from those in urban settings.

While the term Fujizuka describes many mounds, no two are identical in form, and there is a truly fascinating range of structures, elements, historical contexts, and surrounding environments. Observing Fujizuka is fascinating not only for their physical forms but also for their historical and cultural significance, which becomes more evident as we broaden our view to include their surroundings.

Hiroyuki Negishi
Nerima Cultural Promotion Association

References:
1. *Fujizuka in Nerima: Record of Folk-Cultural Properties, Vol. 2*, Nerima Board of Education, 1984.
2. *Shrines in Nerima: Third Revised Edition, Local History Series No. 5*, Nerima Board of Education, 2006.
3. *Mount Fuji in Edo / Tokyo and Nerima*, Nerima Shakujiikoen Furusato Museum, 2015.

(Upper left) Ekoda Fujizuka Location: 1-59-2 Kotake-cho, Nerima, Tokyo, on the grounds of Sengen Shrine, (Upper right) Shimo-Nerima Fujizuka Location: 2-41 Kita-machi, Nerima, Tokyo, on the grounds of Sengen Shrine, (Lower left) Hikawa Shrine Fujizuka Location: 8-22 Kita-machi, Nerima, Tokyo, on the grounds of Hikawa Shrine, (Lower right) Nakazato Fujizuka Location: 1-44 Oizumi-machi, Nerima, Tokyo, next to Yasaka Shrine

平田晃久プロジェクトデータ
Data on Works since 2003

作品名 | Title
所在地 | location
主要用途 | principal use
設計期間 | design period
施工期間 | construction period
proposal／unbuild／progress

安中アートフォーラム プロポーザル案 | Annaka
群馬県安中市 | Annaka, Gunma
コミュニティーセンター、複合施設 | community center
April 2003–August 2003
proposal

House H
大阪府河内長野市 | Kawachinagano, Osaka
住宅 | house
April 2004–June 2004
unbuild

House S
長野県北佐久郡 | Kitasaku, Nagano
住宅 | house
April 2006–September 2006
unbuild

桝屋本店 | Masuya
新潟県上越市 | Joetsu, Niigata
ショールーム、事務所 | showroom, office
May 2005–November 2005
April 2006 –September 2006

Sofu
椅子 | chair
October2006–
–November 2006

R-Minamiaoyama ※1
東京都港区 | Minato-ku, Tokyo
商業施設、事務所 | commercial facility
August 2005–October 2005
December 2005–October 2006

Pleats Principle
原理
January 2007–

Ooder
神奈川県横浜市 | Yokohama, Kanagawa
ヘアサロン | hair salon
May 2006–February 2007
February 2007–April 2007

Ferragamo Bag
バッグ | bag
February 2007–May 2007
proposal

Project K
コテージ | cottage
May 2006–June 2007
unbuild

Sarugaku ※1
東京都渋谷区 | Shibuya-ku, Tokyo
商業施設 | commercial facility
March 2006–January 2007
February 2007–October 2007

Kodama Gallery
東京都港区 | Minato-ku, Tokyo
アートギャラリー | gallery
October 2007–November 2007
November 2007–January 2008

Architecture Farm
台湾 新北 | New Taipei, Taiwan
住宅 | house
November 2007–June 2008
unbuild

Pleated Sky
メキシコ メキシコシティ | Mexico City, Mexco
美術館 | museum
April 2008–July 2008
unbuild

Pavilion C
中国 上海 | Shanghai, China
パビリオン | pavilion
July 2008–August 2008
unbuild

イエノイエ | House of House
神奈川県横浜市 | Yokohama, Kanagawa
インフォメーションセンター | information center
November 2006–July 2008
July 2008–August 2008

Csh
スイス バーゼル | Basel, Switzerland
椅子 | chair
December 2006–January 2007
August 2008–September 2008

Gallery S
東京都中央区
Chuou-ku, Tokyo
ギャラリー、住宅 | gallery, house
May 2007–December 2008
unbuild

Animated Knot
イタリア ミラノ | Milan, Italy
インスタレーション | instalation
November 2008–March 2009
March 2009–April 2009

Flame Frame
東京都江東区 | Koto-ku, Tokyo
インスタレーション、照明 | instalation
September 2008–April 2009
May 2009–July 2009

One-Roof Apartment ※1
新潟県上越市 | Joetsu, Niigata
共同住宅 | apartment house
October 2007–August 2008
September 2008–March 2010

Alp
東京都北区 | Kita-ku, Tokyo
共同住宅 | apartment house
February 2008–February 2009
July 2009–March 2010

Fermented City
都市計画 | urban planning
February 2010–March 2010
unbuild

Prism Liquid
イタリア ミラノ | Milan, Italy
インスタレーション | instalation
November 2009–February 2010
February 2010–April 2010

Tangle Table
スイス バーゼル | Basel, Switzerland
テーブル | table
March 2010–
–April 2010

6/1
東京都港区 | Minato-ku, Tokyo
インスタレーション | instalation
February 2010–March 2010
March 2010–April 2010

Foam Form ※2
台湾 高雄市 | Takao, Taiwan
橋、劇場、オフィス、博物館複合施設 | bridge, theater, office, museum
June 2010–January 2011
proposal

吉岡ライブラリー | Yoshioka Library
東京都文京区 | Bunkyo-ku, Tokyo
文庫 | library
February 2010–October 2010
November 2010–February 2011

Panasonic "Photosynthesis"
イタリア ミラノ | Milano, Italy
インスタレーション | installation
October 2010–February 2011
February 2011–April 2011

庭の中のグリッドの中の庭 | Garden within Grid within Garden
京都府京都市 | Kyoto, Kyoto
図書館、研究施設 | library, laboratory
June 2011–September 2011
proposal

熊本菊水小中学校プロポーザル案 | Kikusui Elementary and Junior High School
熊本県玉名郡 | Tamana, Kumamoto
小中学校 | elementary and junior high school
April 2011–October 2011
proposal

House TT
静岡県富士市 | Fuji, Shizuoka
住宅 | house
October 2011–
unbuild

Bloomberg Pavilion
東京都江東区｜Koto-ku, Tokyo
パビリオン｜pavilion
May 2010–April 2011
May 2011–October 2011

Coil
東京都板橋区｜Itabashi-ku, Tokyo
住宅｜house
July 2010–July 2011
August 2011–November 2011

陸前高田みんなの家｜Home for All ※3
岩手県陸前高田市｜Rikuzentakata, Iwate
集会場｜community space
November 2011–June 2012
July 2012–November 2012

Hotel J
台湾 新北｜New Taipei, Taiwan
ホテル｜hotel
April 2011–May 2012
unbuild

Flow_er
東京都港区｜Minato-ku, Tokyo
インスタレーション｜instalation
January 2012–May 2012
June 2012–July 2012

Mori Trust Garden TORA4
東京都港区｜Minato-ku, Tokyo
仮設店舗｜temporary store
June 2012–February 2013
February 2013–April 2013

LEXUS -amazing flow-
イタリアミラノ｜Milan, Italy
インスタレーション｜instalation
November 2012–February 2013
March 2013–April 2013

Panasonic "Energic Energies"
イタリア ミラノ｜Milan, Italy
インスタレーション｜instalation
November 2012–March 2013
March 2013–April 2013

守山市立浮気保育園｜Green Limb Garden
滋賀県守山市｜Moriyama, Shiga
保育園｜nursary
August 2013–October 2013
proposal

Soil
大阪府河内長野市｜Kawachinagano, Osaka
住宅｜house
December 2013–
unbuild

釜石市復興公営住宅｜Kamaishi City Disaster Recovery Public Housing
岩手県釜石市｜Kamaishi, Iwate
共同住宅｜apartment house
January 2013–January 2014
unbuild

金門フェリーターミナルプロポーザル案｜Invisible Lines
台湾 金面｜Kinmen, Taiwan
フェリーターミナル｜ferry terminal
December 2013–January 2014
proposal

富士山世界遺産センタープロポーザル案｜Cloud and Slope
静岡県富士宮市｜Fujinomiya, Shizuoka
ビジターセンター｜guidance center
January 2014–March 2014
proposal

コトリク｜Kotoriku
東京都目黒区｜Meguro-ku, Tokyo
共同住宅｜apartment house
April 2012–January 2013
July 2013–March 2014

Long Garden
台湾 台北｜Taipei, Taiwan
共同住宅｜condminium
December 2013–August 2014
unbuild

Häm
スイス チューリッヒ｜Zurich, Switzerland
インスタレーション｜instalation
November 2013–August 2014
September 2014–September 2014

台南市美術館 "丘谷之森"｜Museum Forest of Hill Valley ※4
台湾 台南｜Tainan, Taiwan
美術館｜gallery
June 2014–September 2014
proposal

東戸塚教会｜Higashi-Totsuka Church
神奈川県横浜市｜Yokohama, Kanagawa
教会｜church
November 2012–November 2013
January 2014–January 2015

かまいしこども園｜Kamaishi Nursery School
岩手県釜石市｜Kamaishi, Iwate
こども園｜nursery
January 2013–March 2014
April 2014–January 2015

Global Cave
フランス パリ｜Paris, France
コテージ｜cottage
January 2015–
unbuild

Taipei Complex, previous version
台湾 台北｜Taipei, Taiwan
美術館、店舗、レストラン複合施設｜museum, commercial facility, restaurant
June 2011–March 2015
unbuild

Alps Tree
イタリア ウディネ｜Udine, Italy
オフィス｜office
January 2015–March 2015
proposal

Taipei Complex
台湾 台北｜Taipei, Taiwan
美術館、店舗、レストラン複合施設｜museum, shops, restaurants
April 2015–
unbuild

Cloud of the Future
中国香港｜Hong Kong, China
パビリオン｜pavilion
August 2015–
unbuild

Long House
チリ ロスビロス｜Los Vilos, Chile
住宅｜house
September 2011–October 2015
April 2016–
unbuild

Timber Form
東京都港区｜Minato-ku, Tokyo
インスタレーション｜instalation
November 2015–January 2016
unbuild

Fermented House
静岡県富士宮市｜Fujinomiya, Shizuoka
住宅、ショールーム、スタジオ｜house with studio, shop
May 2015–April 2016
unbuild

太田市美術館・図書館｜Art Museum & Library, Ota
群馬県太田市｜Ota, Gunma
図書館、美術館｜library, museum
April 2014–March 2015
May 2015–December 2016

Tree-ness House
東京都豊島区｜Toshima-ku, Tokyo
ギャラリー・共同住宅｜gallery, apartment house
December 2009–September 2015
December 2015–August 2017

宮島客船ターミナルプロポーザル案｜Itsukushima Roof
広島県廿日市市｜Hatsukaichi, Hiroshima
フェリーターミナル｜ferry terminal
May 2016–July 2016
proposal

富富話合｜Taipei Roofs
台湾 台北｜Taipei, Taiwan
物販店舗・共同住宅｜commercial facility, apartment house
February 2013–March 2014
April 2014–October 2017

9hours竹橋｜9h Takebashi
東京都千代田区｜Chiyoda-ku, Tokyo
カプセルホテル｜lodging facility
August   2016–June 2017
June 2017–March 2018

9hours赤坂｜9h Akasaka
東京都港区｜Minato-ku, Tokyo
カプセルホテル｜lodging facility
February 2016–March 2017
April 2017–April 2018

Overlap House
東京都豊島区｜Toshima-ku, Tokyo
共同住宅｜apartment house
May 2016–June 2017
July 2017–May 2018

9hours 浅草｜9h Asakusa
東京都台東区｜Taitou-ku, Tokyo
カプセルホテル｜lodging facility
October2016–September 2017
October 2017–September 2018

9hours 新大阪｜9h Shin-Osaka Station
大阪府大阪市｜Osaka, Osaka
カプセルホテル｜lodging facility
April 2017–October 2017
November 2017–September 2018

9hours 水道橋｜9h Suidobashi
東京都千代田区｜Chiyoda-ku, Tokyo
カプセルホテル｜lodging facility
September 2017–December 2018
January 2019–November 2019

9hours 浜松町｜9h Hamamatsucho
東京都港区｜Minato-ku, Tokyo
カプセルホテル｜lodging facility
April 2017–December 2017
January 2018–February 2020

9hours 半蔵門｜9h Hanzomon
東京都千代田区｜Chiyoda-ku, Tokyo
カプセルホテル｜lodging facility
April 2018–January 2019
February 2019–June 2020

Sendai Tree｜Sendai Tree ※5
宮城県仙台市｜Sendai, Miyagi
庁舎｜city hall
August 2020–December 2020
proposal

八代市民俗伝統芸能伝承館｜Center of Yatsushiro Folk Performing Arts
熊本県八代市｜Yatsushiro, Kumamoto
博物館｜museum
July 2018–September 2019
October 2019–June 2021

Global Bowl
東京都渋谷区｜Shibuya-ku, Tokyo
パビリオン｜pavilion
January 2019–May 2021
June 2021–June 2021

Cloud and Field
静岡県静岡市｜Shizuoka, Shizuoka
図書館｜library
October 2021–February 2022
proposal

からまりタイル｜Karamaritile
愛知県常滑市｜Tokoname, Aichi
タイル｜taile
December 2021–February 2022
February 2022–April 2022

華亞案｜Taoyuan Urban Project
台湾 桃園｜Taoyuan, Taiwan
共同住宅、商業施設、オフィス｜residential complex, comercial facility, office
April 2021–
unbuild

シャイニング・クラウズ｜Shining Clouds
島根県松江市｜Matsue, Shimane
住宅｜house
October 2018–November 2021
January 2022–November 2022

Fermented Tower
台湾 桃園｜Taoyuan, Taiwan
共同住宅｜residential complex
April 2013–December 2019
January 2020–December 2022

OTA lines
群馬県太田市｜Ota, Gunma
オフィス、レストラン、ギャラリー｜office, restaurant, gallery
July 2020–December 2021
February 2022–January 2023

ジンズ豊川｜JINS Toyokawa
愛知県豊川市｜Toyokawa, Aichi
店舗｜shop
September 2022–February 2023
February 2023–March 2023

伊勢遺跡史跡公園展示施設｜Ise Remain Heritage Center
滋賀県守山市｜Moriyama, Shiga
博物館｜museum
October 2020–March 2022
June 2022–May 2023

まえばしガレリア｜Maebashi Galleria
群馬県前橋市｜Maebashi, Gunma
共同住宅、商業施設｜apartment house, commercial facility
January 2020–December 2021
January 2022–May 2023

Ryozan Park Green
東京都豊島区｜Toshima-ku, Tokyo
共同住宅｜apartment house
December 2020–August 2022
August 2022–February 2024

HARAKADO
東京都渋谷区｜Shibuya-ku, Tokyo
商業施設｜commercial facility
February 2016–November 2020
December 2020–August 2023

ホントカ。小千谷市ひと・まち・文化共創拠点｜HONTOKA。Ojiya City People, Town, Cultural Co-creation Base
新潟県小千谷市｜Ojiya, Niigata
図書館、複合施設｜library complex
April 2021–June 2022
November 2022–September 2024

Ota Complex
群馬県太田市｜Ota, Gunma
図書館、保健センター、行政センター｜library, health center, administration center
May 2021–October 2022
January 2023–
progress

EXPO ナショナルデーホール「レイガーデン」※5｜EXPO National Day Hall "Ray Garden"
大阪府大阪市｜Osaka, Osaka
ホール、展示場、ラウンジ｜hall, gallery, lounge
November 2021–October 2023
December 2023–
progress

内湖集合住宅｜Neihu Apartment
台湾 台北｜Taipei, Taiwan
共同住宅｜apartment house
May 2022–May 2024
June 2024–
progress

HARAJUKU Stairs
東京都渋谷区｜Shibuya-ku, Tokyo
商業施設｜commercial facility
April 2020–April 2024
May 2024–
progress

新竹市中央図書館｜Knowledge Canyon ※6
台湾 新竹｜Hsinchu, Taiwan
図書館、オフィス｜library, office
September 2019–March 2020
June 2020–
progress

臺灣大學 藝文大樓｜Theater, Art Gallery and Museum of Taiwan university ※7
台湾 台北｜Taipei, Taiwan
博物館、美術館、劇場、宿泊施設、オフィス｜museum, art gallery, theater, accommodation, office
January 2023–
progress

基隆路プロジェクト｜Keelung Rd project
台湾 台北｜Taipei, Taiwan
共同住宅、商業施設、オフィス｜apartment house, commercial facility, office
September 2023–
progress

BIG-TREE ※8
山形県山形市｜Yamagata, Yamagata
コンサートホール｜concert hall
August 2024–
progress

練馬区立美術館・貫井図書館｜Nerima Art Museum and Nukui Library
東京都練馬区｜Nerima-ku, Tokyo
美術館、図書館｜museum, library
January2023–
progress

※1 吉原美比古と共同設計
※2 劉培森建築師事務所と共同設計
※3 伊東豊雄、畠山直哉、乾久美子、藤本壮介と協働
※4 張瑪龍陳玉霖聯合建築師事務所と共同設計
※5 株式会社安井建築設計事務所と共同設計
※6 郭旭原聯合建築師事務所と共同設計
※7 黄翔龍建築師事務所と共同設計
※8 株式会社安井建築設計事務所、株式会社平吹設計事務所、
　　株式会社鈴木建築設計事務所と共同設計
　　協力：アクアパルス建築設計事務所

平田 晃久（ひらた あきひさ）

建築家、京都大学教授

■ 略歴

1971年　大阪府に生まれる
1997年　京都大学工学研究科修了
　　　　伊東豊雄建築設計事務所
2005年　平田晃久建築設計事務所設立
2015年　京都大学大学院准教授
2018年　京都大学大学院教授

■ 受賞歴

2022年　日本建築学会賞
2020年　GOLDEN PIN DESIGN AWARD 2020
2018年　BCS賞
2018年　村野藤吾賞
2015年　日本建築設計学会賞
2012年　第13回ヴェネチア・ビエンナーレ国際建築展日本館展示金獅子賞*
2012年　ELITA DESIGN AWARD
2008年　第19回JIA新人賞
2004年　SDレビュー朝倉賞**

* 伊東豊雄、畠山直哉、乾久美子、藤本壮介と協働受賞
**伊東豊雄建築設計事務所在籍時の個人プロジェクト

Photo: Marc Goodwin, Archmospheres

Akihisa HIRATA

Architect, Professor at Kyoto University

1971	Born in Osaka, Japan
1997	Recieved a master's degree from the Kyoto University Graduate School of Engineering
	Worked at Toyo Ito & Associates, Architects
2005	Established akihisa hirata architecture office
2015	Associates professor at Kyoto University
2018	Professor at Kyoto University

■ Awards

2022	AIJ Prize 2022
2020	GOLDEN PIN DESIGN AWARD 2020
2018	BCS Prize
2018	Murano Togo Prize
2015	Architectural Design Associates of Nippon Prize
2012	ELITA DESIGN AWARD (Best of Milano Salone)
2012	Golden Lion at the 13th International Architecture Exhibition - La Biennale di Venezia*
2008	JIA New Face Award
2004	Asakura Award of SD Review**

* "Architecture, Possible here?" worked with Toyo Ito, Naoya Hatakeyama, Kumiko Inui and Sou Fujimoto
**Personal project during at Toyo Ito & Associates, Architects

Current Staff Members

平田晃久	|	Akihisa Hirata
外木裕子	|	Yuko Tonogi
杉山征利	|	Masatoshi Sugiyama
青山 稔	|	Minoru Aoyama
市古 慧	|	Kei Ichigo
渋谷 黎	|	Rei Shibuya
西里正敏	|	Masatoshi Nishizato
北島瑛登	|	Eito Kitajima
吉村真菜	|	Mana Yoshimura
山口大樹	|	Daiki Yamaguchi
花輪優香	|	Yuka Hanawa
高橋あかね	|	Akane Takahashi
長谷川 峻	|	Shun Hasegawa
久連松文乃	|	Ayano Kurematsu
大澤稔里	|	Minori Osawa
山田寛太	|	Kanta Yamada
彭 莞浄	|	Peng Wanjing
清武優子	|	Yuko Kiyotake
張 仕林	|	Zhang Shilin
大室 新	|	Arata Omuro
谷本かな穂	|	Kanaho Tanimoto
葉 運祺	|	Yeh Yun-Chih
大宮由紀子	|	Yukiko Omiya

謝辞

Acknowledgments

本展覧会の開催ならびに本書の刊行にあたりまして、多大なご協力を賜りました皆様、貴重な作品や資料を快くご出品くださった各施設、ご所蔵家の方々、そして様々な面でご協力いただきました関係者の皆様方に、厚く御礼申し上げます。（五十音順・敬称略）

We would like to express our deep gratitude to everyone for their considerable support, as well as to all museums, companies and private owners who willingly provided items from their valuable collections, and to everyone else who contributed in one way or another to the realization of this exhibition and the publication of this catalogue.

雨宮透貴	Yukitaka Amemiya
アルティ株式会社	arti Inc.
安東陽子	Yoko Ando
岩﨑茂	Shigeru Iwasaki
遠藤豊	Yutaka Endo
尾形万里子	Mariko Ogata
小千谷市にぎわい交流課	Ojiya City Lively Exchange Division
株式会社STRUKT	STRUKT Co., Ltd.
株式会社東京スタデオ	TOKYO STUDIO Co., LTD.
株式会社DOTWORKS	DOTWORKS Inc.
株式会社BIG-TREE	BIG-TREE Co., Ltd
株式会社リクシル	LIXIL Corporation
黒川貴	Takashi Kurokawa
白井雅明	Masaaki Shirai
瀬戸山雅彦	Masahiko Setoyama
タカ・イシイギャラリー	Taka Ishii Gallery
高野淳一	Junichi Takano
高橋大樹	Daiki Takahashi
都築恵美子	Emiko Tsuzuki
TOTO出版	TOTO Publishing
成定由香沙	Yukasa Narisada
練馬区立石神井公園ふるさと文化館	Nerima Shakujiikoen Furusato Museum
伴野幸一	Koichi Banno
璞園建築團隊	Pauian Archiland
宮崎悦男	Etsuo Miyazaki
守山市伊勢遺跡史跡公園	Moriyama City Ise Site Historic Park
守山市教育委員会	Moriyama City Board of Education
守山市立埋蔵文化財センター	Moriyama City Archaeological Culture Center

本書は「平田晃久—人間の波打ちぎわ」展の公式図録兼書籍として刊行されました。

平田晃久
—人間の波打ちぎわ

練馬区立美術館
2024年7月28日（日）—9月23日（月・休）

主催：練馬区立美術館（公益財団法人練馬区文化振興協会）
後援：一般社団法人日本建築学会、公益財団法人日本建築家協会
助成：NOMURA 野村財団
協賛：株式会社シェルター、株式会社オカムラ、ケイミュー株式会社、大光電機株式会社、
　　　鹿島建設株式会社、株式会社竹中工務店、清水建設株式会社

展示構成：平田晃久建築設計事務所
学芸担当：小野寛子（練馬区立美術館）
広報・管理担当：佐藤秋乃（練馬区立美術館）
広報物デザイン：近藤一弥
平田晃久建築設計事務所（展示・図録担当）：高橋あかね、長谷川峻、大澤稔里、山田寛太

This book was published as the official catalogue of the "Akihisa Hirata: Architecture Arises at the Water's Edge foe Humans" exhibition.

Akihisa Hirata:
Architecture Arises at the Water's Edge for Humans

Nerima Art Museum, Tokyo
July 28-September 23, 2024

Organized by Nerima Art Museum/Nerima Cultural Promotion Association
Under the Auspices of Architectural Institute of Japan, The Japan Institute of Architects
Supported by Nomura Foundation
Sponsored by Shelter Co., Ltd, OKAMURA CORPORATION, KMEW Co., Ltd, DAIKO ELECTRIC Co.,Ltd, KAJIMA CORPORATION, TAKENAKA CORPORATION, SHIMIZU CORPORATION

Planned by akihisa hirata architecture office
Curated by Hiroko Ono（Nerima Art Museum）
Coordinated by Akino Sato (Nerima Art Museum)
Publicity Design: Kazuya Kondo
akihisa hirata architecture office (staff in charge of the exhibition and catalogue):
Akane Takahashi, Shun Hasegawa, Minori Osawa, Kanta Yamada

執筆：西沢立衛、伊東正伸（練馬区立美術館）、
小野寛子（練馬区立美術館）、根岸博之（公益財団法人練馬区文化振興協会）

企画：練馬区立美術館
プロデューサー：東浜薄夫

編集：平田晃久建築設計事務所、小野寛子、古屋歴（青幻舎）
翻訳：川上純子、クリストファー・スティヴンズ
ブックデザイン：林琢真（林琢真デザイン事務所）
表紙：外木裕子（平田晃久建築設計事務所）

Credits:
Akihisa Hirata: 19, 25, 28, 33, 38, 71, 74, 79, 88, 96 (tracing paper), 102-103, 116, 122
Cameron Beccario, earth.nullschool.net (Base image): 113
Daici Ano: 58-59, 69, 70, 72-73, 80-81, 86-87, 90-93
ICHIKAWA Yasushi: 97-101
Kenya Chiba: 76-77
KKOP Co.Ltd. Kenta Hasegawa: 94-95
Koichi Torimura: 104-107, 129-131
Marc Goodwin, Archmospheres: 165
Nacása & Partners Inc.: 16-17
Shinkenchiku-sha: 42-43, 84-85
Shinya Kigure+Lo.cul.p: 60-61
Takumi Ota: 24, 26
ToLoLo studio: 30-31
Vincent Hecht: 40-41
YASHIRO PHOTO OFFICE: 78
Yukasa Narisada: 62-63, 64-68
Yukikazu Ito: 44-45
Yukitaka Amemiya: 1, 137-145

特記なきものは平田晃久建築設計事務所の提供による
Unless otherwise indicated here, photographs and other related materials were
provided by akihisa hirata architecture office

Text: Ryue Nishizawa, Masanobu Ito (Nerima Art Museum),
Hiroko Ono (Nerima Art Museum), Hiroyuki Negishi (Nerima Cultural Promotion Association)

Concept: Nerima Art Museum
Produced by Usuo Higashihama

Edit: akihisa hirata architecture office, Hiroko Ono,
Ayumi Furuya (Seigensha Art Publishing, Inc.)
Translation: Junko Kawakami, Christopher Stephens
Book Design: Takuma Hayashi (HAYASHI TAKUMA DESIGN OFFICE)
Cover Graphic: Yuko Tonogi (akihisa hirata architecture office)

平田晃久
―人間の波打ちぎわ

発行日：2024年8月31日　初版発行

編著：平田晃久

発行者：片山誠
発行所：株式会社青幻舎
京都市中京区梅忠町9-1 〒604-8136
Tel. 075-252-6766
Fax. 075-252-6770
https://www.seigensha.com

印刷・製本：株式会社サンエムカラー

©AKIHISA HIRATA, Nerima Art Museum 2024, Printed in Japan
ISBN978-4-86152-960-3 C0052

本書のコピー、スキャン、デジタル化等の無断複製は、著作権法上での例外を除き禁じられて
います。

AKIHISA HIRATA
Architecture Arises at the Water's Edge for Humans

First edition: August 31, 2024

Edited by Akihisa Hirata

Publisher: Makoto Katayama
Published by Seigensha Art Publishing Inc.
9-1, Umetada-cho, Nakagyo-ku, Kyoto, 604-8136, Japan
Tel. +81-75-252-6766
Fax. +81-75-252-6770
https://www.seigensha.com

Printed and Bound by SunM Color Co., Ltd.

©AKIHISA HIRATA, Nerima Art Museum 2024, Printed in Japan
ISBN978-4-86152-960-3 C0052

All right reserved. No part of this publication may be reproduced without written
permission.